PEOPLE, TIME & MONEY
VOLUME 2

INSIGHTFUL MANAGEMENT TIPS
FOR SUCCESSFUL ENTREPRENEURS

RICH RUSSAKOFF

BOTTOM LINE UP ENTERPRISES, LLC.

Editing by Gena Kenny, Siobhan Casey, and Rachel Weisberg

Front cover image created by Mexelina and Lucy Martinez

Book design by Siobhan Casey

Published by Bottom Line Up Enterprises, LLC.

60114 Davie, Chapel Hill, NC 27517

Visit www.coachtothebest.com

This book is dedicated to my parents, Arthur and Lillian Russakoff, my wife, Maureen "Moe" McBride-Russakoff, the hundreds of entrepreneurs I've worked with throughout my career, as well as my friends and supporters in the Food For Thought community.

LAUNCHING PEOPLE, TIME & MONEY VOLUME ONE

In June of 2021, *People, Time & Money, Volume 1* was published. There was a lengthy list of action items to be done in preparation. Some of which included:

- Finalize the list of people we will ask to review it
- Populate the Amazon Author Page
- Create social media graphics to promote the book over the launch week
- Work on the media kit
- Launch the book to Kindle

I will never forget what went through my mind as I began working on a dedication for the book. Without question, I dedicated the book to my parents, to Moe, and to the hundreds of entrepreneurs I've worked with throughout my career.

From the time I could contribute, I worked in my parent's dry cleaning business during summers, holidays, and on Saturdays. My parents taught me a good work ethic, how to take calculated risks, how to treat employees, and how to always give customers a great product.

I learned from them how to deal with hardships and downturns, with courage and resilience. They also instilled in me values that I use in my coaching practice to this day, such as:

- Treat people with respect
- Create opportunities for people to grow
- Be true to your word
- Don't burn bridges
- Pay it forward

When my parents came to visit my first retail business, I had a dozen questions prepared to ask my dad regarding upcoming decisions. In virtually every case he said, "Son, go with your gut." Eventually, it sunk in that he was saying, "I trust you to make the right decisions; when you make wrong ones, you'll learn from them. And as a business owner, you need to be decisive."

I want to thank Moe for believing in me and encouraging me to write and share what I have learned over my fifty-year career. Moe does a thousand things a week to help me. She introduced me to Gay Hendricks, which led us to become Big Leap and Conscious Loving coaches. She has assembled a great team, including Lucy Martinez, our Branding and Marketing Director, and my writing coach, Siobhan Casey, who were invaluable in making the first volume happen.

There is an old saying that a consultant is someone who borrows your watch to tell you the time and then gets to keep the watch. That means an entrepreneur gives you their watch, which is their problem, and the coach tells them the time, offering them a solution. The coach gets to keep 'the watch' or the solution to add to their bank of wisdom.

A great coach does not measure their success in how much money they've made, but in how many watches they have. So, thank you to all the entrepreneurs that gave me their watches. These include entrepreneurs like Brett Hatton, who took me all over the world, Damon Gersh, who I've coached and remained a close friend with for over twenty years, and Daniel Marcus. I could name at least one hundred more who have made my job and my life more meaningful.

I'd also like to dedicate this book and volume one to Jim Woods of INC Magazines coaching division, who believed in me and opened countless doors, including my introduction to The Entrepreneurial Organization (EO).

Thank you, Verne Harnish, who included me in his book *Mastering the Rockefeller's Habits* and brought me back every year to speak at what is now The Entrepreneurial Master's Program educational program for business owners. Thank you also to Brian Brault, who gave me the opportunity to share my "Taking Your Big Leap" presentation at the Entrepreneurial Master's Program held at Massachusetts Institute of Technology, which I have since presented to Entrepreneurial Organization chapters in Mexico, Australia, Nepal, and throughout the USA. Brian has become a spiritual soulmate of mine.

And to the Food for Thought community, who have encouraged me to continue writing about my journey and what I learn from entrepreneurs every day.

Finally, I dedicate this book to every entrepreneur who has fought the good fight, experienced the blood, sweat, and tears that go with the territory, and survived to make their dreams and vision become a reality. It isn't easy, it's a roller coaster ride, but it sure is worth it.

FIFTY YEARS OF EXPERIENCES, TWO YEARS IN THE MAKING, ONE DAY AT A TIME, AND VOILA - PEOPLE, TIME AND MONEY IS A BOOK

Writing has given me a newfound self-confidence and has allowed me to share stories that date back from my early childhood to what is happening today.

I urge everyone to write. The writer's mantra is to write it, then get it right, but write it. It's an incredible learning opportunity. First for the writer and then for the reader. My daily email posts, and this book, allow me to reach more people than I could in my primary role as a coach and a speaker. So, I'm dedicating the time to continue writing and sharing the wisdom and insights I have learned from my work-life experiences over the last 50 years.

So how do you write a book with 73 different stories and messages?

- The first step is to commit to writing.
- Find a writing coach who can help you construct and deconstruct your writing.
- Use writing tools like Grammarly. (NOTE: Grammarly won't catch a geographical error - like writing that Little Italy is in Brooklyn, not New York City, nor will it catch numerical errors, if you mean $2.99 per gallon and write $299 instead - we need to pay attention to these accuracies ourselves).

- Write every day and listen to the feedback you receive.
- Always be looking for a story, a challenge, or a lesson learned.
- Recognize that everything you write may be a gift or inspiration for someone.
- In time you will develop your unique style.
- Don't be afraid to make mistakes.
- To be authentic, you must be willing to be vulnerable.
- Take risks - write about what's important to you.
- Writing something every day makes you a better listener, thinker, and opportunist - I'm always looking for a subject for a future post.
- Some of my best posts have been created at 8PM the night before. When I finally decide on a message or story I want to share, it's like a revelation.
- Friday's Best of Food for Thought posts allows me to revisit posts I've written over a year ago and see how I can make them better.

Since I started writing in September 2019, I have learned my craft. After I published *People, Time & Money Volume One*, I started taping the audio version, which was a throwback to my radio days. Sometime down the road, we'll have a Spanish translation of each of my books. Time permitting, I will write a business fable and publish several more books, and I'll do it one day at a time.

DO WHAT MAKES YOU HAPPY

A man once said to a Buddhist monk, "I want happiness."
The monk smiled softly and said, "First remove 'I' - that is your ego.
Then remove 'want' – that is your unending desire.
Now all you are left with (and were born with) is 'happiness'." - Anonymous

When I was in grade school, my second-grade teacher, Mrs. Pancoast, gave us a homework assignment of writing what we wanted to be when we grew up. I wrote that I wanted to be happy. I described happiness as living in a lovely home with a wonderful loving partner.

She gave me a failing grade for not taking the assignment seriously. Yes, that's right, I didn't take being happy seriously. There was no convincing her otherwise.

In April of 2022, I will celebrate my 77th birthday. As I look back, I wouldn't change a thing I wrote, and I've never been happier. Wherever you are, Mrs. Pancoast, I'm happy to report your failing grade did not deter me in my pursuit of happiness.

Rule #1. Do what makes you happy.

THIS IS THE WAY WE DO BUSINESS

D on't expect people to have your vision if you don't make it clear. To establish the culture and the customer experience you desire, you must teach your team these three things:

1. HOW you do business
2. WHY it's essential
3. HOW TO TAKE RESPONSIBILITY for maintaining the behaviors that drive the customer experience.

In my first business, every season during orientation, we ensured that everyone on our staff understood the following were non-negotiable:

1. The Greeting
2. Create Interest
3. The Rule
4. Making the Sale
5. There are Six Ways to Buy
6. Know When to Stop
7. How We Do Business

The Greeting

We greeted every new customer with the following welcome:

"Welcome to R&R; just about everything we carry is handmade. If you'd like to know who made it, where it's from, or how it's made, all you have to do is ask."

Why is it important?

We wanted all customers to be greeted warmly. If someone came in with the intention to steal, they would immediately know we had established eye contact with them. We encouraged questions, and we gave three safe questions to ask.

Create Interest

If a customer was looking at a piece of jewelry, we would take it out of the case and tell them about the history of the piece, the artist that made it, and the provenance or country of origin.

Why is it important?

You can't sell jewelry if it's in a case. We waited for the customer to show interest, then we took it out of the case, bringing the item closer for their inspection. Our goal was to engage the customer not by "telling" but by "selling." We would invite them to try it on. This created the opportunity for the customer to "sell themselves." We offered them alternative options and showed them other selections for them to consider or to compare.

The Rule

As a rule, we never took out more than three pieces at a time.

Why is it important?

A professional thief wants you to lose count of what you are showing. They will distract you so they can slip a piece of jewelry into their pocket. So, if we took a fourth piece, we would put one back in the case, always having, at most, three pieces out.

Making the Sale

ASK the customer, "Do you like it?" If they said yes, we followed up with, "Would you like to buy it?"

Why is it important?

Sales 101 - Ask for the order.

Make it Easy to Buy

It is important to make it as easy as possible for the customer to buy something. We accepted 6 different forms of payment: Cash, checks, AMEX, Visa, Mastercard and we allowed layaway.

Why is it important?

Our job is to make it easy for them to purchase things!

Know When to Stop

Once the buyer says yes, stop selling! Now it's time to reassure them they made a great choice.

Why is it important?

All salespeople must understand that what the big mouth giveth the big mouth can take away. Now is the time to reassure the customer that they made a good choice and you're happy for them.

Accountability

If you see someone shortcutting or ignoring "how we do business", it's your job or the managers to hold team members accountable for the integrity of "how we do business."

Why is it important?

You must continue to reinforce to your team:

1. That this is how we do business.
2. Why it's essential.

3. That there are consequences for not following how we maintain our customer experience.

It doesn't matter if you're in a manufacturing, product, or service business, it's critical to create the customer experience you desire and hold your team accountable for "how you do business."

THE 10 GIFTS OF COACHING

"A good coach will make his players see what they can be rather than what they are." - Ara Parasheghian

Great coaches help you make better decisions and give you perspective. Paying a coach won't make you a great entrepreneur – listening to one will.

About twenty years ago, I came across an article in an issue of *Runner's World* that listed the following 10 attributes of a great coach:

1. **Motivation** - Coaches can motivate you to be your best self and to take calculated risks for business and personal growth.

2. **Systems** - Coaches suggest systems and rhythms so you can be more productive.

3. **Goal Setting** - Coaches help you establish the right goals for you and hold you accountable for the actions that will achieve them.

4. **Advice** - Coaches give you advice and guidance to make the best decisions. Sometimes the best choice is to pass on an opportunity. A coach won't let you rush to failure.

5. **Burnout Prevention** - A great coach will insist that you take vaca-

tions and breaks so you remain sharp, fresh, and creative. We all need to recharge.

In the book *The Power of Full Engagement,* authors Tony Schwartz and Jim Loehr tell us that life is not a marathon; it is a continuing process of sprints and recovery. A coach encourages you to put your time and energy into doing the activities you enjoy and do best, so you don't burn out. A coach will discourage you from getting caught up in the thick of thin things.

6. **Plateau-Busting** - A great coach encourages you to strive for higher goals and guides you on making them happen. They teach you how to be a better leader and how to delegate but not abdicate.

7. **Checklists** - Coaches provide you with checklists that enable you to focus on your priorities and not let important things fall through the cracks.

8. **Feedback** - Great coaches are your sounding board to give you honest advice that can only come from experience. They commit to listening and understanding, and they tell you what you need to hear, which is not always what you want to hear.

9. **Cheerleader** - As a coach, I consider myself the CEO's CEO or "Chief Encouragement Officer." We all need encouragement and praise and someone to say "Damn good job" when we do a damn good job. We also need someone to lift us when things don't go our way, to remind us that there will be another day, and to help us see the valuable learning opportunities from temporary failures.

10. **Balance** - A coach reminds you to make life fun and enjoy the journey, and they remind you to not neglect your health, your family, or the activities that restore your soul.

As a coach, I have learned that the most coachable people are lifetime learners who have humility, want to be the best they can be, and listen and act when they have the clarity to their best path. That is what makes coaching so fulfilling.

Coach wishes you a splendid day.

BEHAVIORS ARE THE LEADING INDICATORS OF RESULTS

Leading indicators define what actions are necessary to achieve our goals with measurable outcomes. They "lead" to successfully meeting overall business objectives.

While presenting at an Entrepreneurial Master's Program several years ago, one participant shared how he onboards salespeople to maximize their success.

He gives each new salesperson specific key performance indicators (KPIs) to create leads that would ultimately generate sales.

For the first 90 days, he would build these KPIs into the salesperson's compensation structure. The goal is to ensure a salesperson commits to the behaviors necessary to succeed. If they meet their KPI goals, they receive an additional 30% performance bonus. If not, they may lose the opportunity to work for the company.

I urge every company to consider the following approach for onboarding a Business-to-Business sales candidate.

Phase 1 - Training and Orientation

1. Teach the salesperson how to sell your product or service and how to overcome common objections from buyers.
2. Teach them your company's values, why they are crucial to your culture, and how you do business.
3. Provide the salesperson with a clear understanding of the profile of your target clients and share case studies of happy clients.
4. If you have a list of target companies to prospect, walk them through it. If not, share with them how to create one. There are many ways to identify opportunities, including LinkedIn, trade publications, and referrals. A resourceful salesperson will use them all.
5. Make sure they are clear on who uses, chooses, benefits from, and buys your products or services—i.e., who must say yes, and who writes the checks.
6. Roleplay with them how to make a cold call, write an email, or make a presentation.

Phase 2 - Identify and Implement the KPI's

- If it takes ten contacts to generate one lead, the first KPI is how many contacts you have attempted to reach. Set a realistic number as the KPI.
- The second KPI is how many contacts you reached as a percentage of a specific goal. For example, if the goal is to reach 70 contacts a week and we successfully reach 63, the result of the second KPI is 90%.
- The third KPI is how many contacts you have with each identified prospect.
- Let's say, on average, it takes ten contacts to turn a lead into a client, then how many contacts have you made per prospect?
- How many warm leads do you have?
- How many hot leads do you have?
- How many deals closed and resulted in a sale?

In sales, the key to success is focus, consistency, and mastering the art of telling a story, not selling a product. A customer is more likely to buy if they feel they are being spoken to at their level, rather than being sold a pitch. If a salesperson implements the behaviors necessary for success, everyone wins. It's our job to give them the tools, training, and path to success.

Within 90 days or less, you'll know if you've hired the right salesperson. If not, you'll know you've given them every opportunity to succeed.

THE FIVE ACCOUNTABILITY CHALLENGES EVERY BUSINESS MUST MASTER

"Wisdom is knowing the right path to take. Integrity is taking it." - M.H. McKee

All the planning, initiatives, personnel, and invested money are meaningless if a company does not execute and achieve measurable results.

It's not just the CEO and the COO's job to ensure results. In the best of cultures, everyone takes responsibility to hold themselves accountable for the mission, goals, standards, and actions that the company has established.

I'm not sure where I found these critical questions companies must answer, but I think it's from Pat Lencioni's classic book *The Five Dysfunctions of a Team.*

I encourage every leadership team to answer these questions in a workshop and determine what you are doing well and where you need to improve. There is a lot to assess, so it may be best to take on one at a time.

I have added a few talking points with each question to get you started.

16

1. How do we ensure that projects within areas of specific responsibility are completed on time and within budget?

One person must own every project from start to finish. Do you have a template for the budget, steps, stages, and personnel necessary to complete projects? I recommend reading *Execution, the Discipline of Getting Things Done*, by Larry Bossidy and Ram Charan for more information on this.

Does each project have timelines and milestones established before the launch?

Do you have a Plan B in case the project plan or mission is not feasible?

2. How do we provide feedback that is clear and direct?

Start with taking the time to make sure everyone is clear on their roles and responsibilities. Make paraphrasing, where an individual repeats back what is being asked of them in their own words, a part of all communications.

Be honest and not afraid to hold someone accountable. Read *Crucial Conversations* by Kerry Patterson, Al Switzler, Joseph Grenny, Emily Gregory, and Ron McMillan.

There must be consequences for repeated behaviors that are detrimental to the company's objectives and values.

Remember that honesty without compassion is cruelty.

Praise in public, criticize in private.

3. How do we ensure the quality, accuracy, and completeness of work activities?

Systems and processes must be in place to minimize mistakes and maximize efficiency. Everyone who touches the process must make sure that they sign off and pass it on error-free.

Create KPIs to measure quality, accuracy, and completeness. Anything less than your highest standards is a red flag that must be identified and corrected immediately.

Follow-through is the secret to successful execution.

4. How do we develop individual team members to maximize their abilities and talents?

Hire people who are committed to high performance and results, and who work well with others. Use services like DiSC, The Predictive Index, and Culture Index to help determine if the candidate has the best profile for the position.

Bradford Smart's 3rd edition of *Topgrading* is an invaluable tool to make an art of your hiring practices.

My mantra is, "Hire the best, fire the pests. You are in the hiring, inspiring, requiring, firing, training, and communications business."

A company is only as good as its people. There is no room for interior terrorists, regardless of how good their skills are.

Don't set people up for failure. Put the right people in the right seat and give them the tools and training they need to excel.

5. How do we maintain a productive working relationship with team members?

Listen to your team members, keep them in the loop, ask for feedback, and recognize and praise outstanding performance. Make sure everyone is clear on their roles and responsibilities. Praise (when earned) is the fuel that drives performance.

"WHAT'S IN A NAME?"

⁂

"THAT WHICH WE CALL A ROSE / BY ANY OTHER NAME WOULD SMELL AS SWEET."

M ost of us know these famous words by heart. If perchance you don't, the lines are from Shakespeare's *Romeo and Juliet*. Juliet, quoted above, says this to Romeo about his family name, Montague. The Montagues and the Capulets, Juliet's family, were bitter enemies.

So, "What's in a name? That which we call a rose by any other name would smell as sweet." Well, maybe not. Maybe a rose would smell sweeter by another name.

When I founded my coaching business in the mid-eighties, I named it Bottom Line Consultants. Today when I'm referred to as a consultant, I cringe. A *consultant* is more aloof, analytical, and focused on policy, trends, and processes. If you want "a study," then hire a consultant. The word *consultant* feels cold and distant to me. Perhaps it's because a professional consultant does studies and tries to present facts to back up their analysis.

The word *coach* feels warm and intimate to me; someone who is focused on individuals and team building. If you are seeking personal and team growth, hire a coach. When my clients call me coach, I feel pride and connection. However, both the role of the consultant and the coach have their place.

Many years ago, *Millionaire Magazine* wrote an extensive profile about me, entitled "Coach to the Best."

The title resonated with me. So, we changed the company name to "Coach to the Best." The best entrepreneurs are lifetime learners and are all about being of service to their team and their clients equally. What makes them "The Best"? It's their desire to continue to grow (themselves and their team members), coupled with a strong dose of humility.

They may not start out as the best, but they have the "best attitude", and they empower themselves to become *their* best. "The Best" understand that it's an eternal journey and they thrive on it.

Being "Coach to the Best" for me is a much sweeter name than "Rich Russakoff, Consultant." No disrespect to Romeo and Juliet, but perhaps by changing their names from Montagues and Capulets to true lovers, they would smell even sweeter.

BEWARE OF INTERIOR TERRORISTS AND SET YOURSELF FREE

❦

"Nothing is certain but death and taxes." - Benjamin Franklin

While Ben Franklin may have been right, it's also certain that sooner or later, most companies find they have an interior terrorist in their midst.

An interior terrorist is someone who, by their attitude or behaviors, negatively impacts:

- The work of others
- The company culture
- The client experience

The actions of the company or a manager may cause a change in someone's behavior. In the words of Marcus Buckingham, "**People leave managers, not companies.**"

Below is a list of the many actions and attitudes that I have seen result in toxicity in a company. Sadly, there's a real person, company, and story behind each example.

- They believe they are your savior and the only ones who can protect you from the big bad boss.
- They thrive on creating chaos.
- They are insecure.
- They maintain their power by dividing the two owners and "playing one against the other."
- The owners set unrealistic expectations, and they feel justified and are happy to stir everyone up by talking about them behind their backs.
- They need to be loved more than respected, so they don't hold others accountable.
- They are troubled in their personal life and take it out at work.
- They are bullies that get off humiliating others, which can result in good people quitting.
- They spread the word that the boss is spending way too much money in the wrong places.
- They believe they are the smartest guy in the room, and that if they were running the company EVERYTHING would be better. (Never mind that they are not risk-takers and that it's easier to criticize than to steer the ship).
- They are jealous of the CEO or other team leaders.
- They have an inflated ego.
- They are angry because they believe they should be making more money.
- They have issues that have nothing to do with the business.
- They want to be the hero, so they tell others, "The CEO is exploiting you, but I've got your back."
- They are managers who tell their team, "The boss is stupid, and if I were running the department the way I want, we would be far more productive."
- They are leaders who tell everyone in the company how overwhelmed they are.
- They are in over their heads and blame others for their shortcomings.

Negativity and drama are as contagious as a fire out of control.

If you have an interior terrorist, I strongly recommend letting them go as soon as you have a replacement or a plan B.

Depending on the circumstances, you may not always have the luxury of time, and if you don't, choose sooner rather than later. Pull the trigger ASAP.

Don't worry about what your team members will think. In my experience, most will say, "What took you so long?"

"There are some people who always seem angry and continuously look for conflict. Walk away; the battle they are fighting isn't with you, it is with themselves." - Anonymous

QUESTIONS TO ASK ABOUT A COACH OR PROFESSIONAL ADVISOR

Recently I asked a prospective client if it would help him to call some of my current clients for references before making his decision on engaging in a coaching relationship with me. "Yes," he said, "But I have no idea what to ask."

The questions I suggested included:

1. How does he help you?
2. What are some of the issues you are comfortable sharing that he's helped you resolve?
3. What are the things you're working on with him now?
4. Is he a good listener?
5. Does he share information in a way you can understand?
6. Does he call you out when you need to be called out?
7. Does he encourage you?
8. Does he call you when he finds something to share, such as information he thinks you will find valuable?
9. Have you grown as a result of the relationship?
10. If you had to do it all over again, would you?
11. Are you getting the value for your money?
12. Is there anything he could do better?

13. Does he cut you off when you schedule for an hour, and you need more time?
14. How fast does he return your calls, emails, and text messages?

During the ten years I lived in Austin, I was fortunate to have Dr. John Murray as my physician, and recently Dr. Todd Granger in Chapel Hill. Along with our accountant, Anita Savoy, they each receive the highest grade on these questions.

These questions are good to ask about any professional service provider and can serve as a barometer for you to assess your trusted advisors. Be sure you get the service and attention you're paying for. And, if you are a professional advisor, it's an excellent checklist to live by.

Make today the day you are a professional in everything you do.

THE POWER OF EMPATHY

B rené Brown, the author of *Atlas of the Heart*, describes empathy as "simply listening, holding space, withholding judgment, emotionally connecting, and communicating that incredibly healing message that you're not alone."

Empathy is crucial because it helps us understand how others are feeling and to respond appropriately. We cannot control the behavior of others, but we can always control how we respond to them.

Perhaps the best thing you can do is to acknowledge how the other person feels.

- Acknowledge their pain
- Show genuine interest
- Be encouraging
- Be supportive

There is opportunity and challenge in knowing when and how to offer your empathy. Empathy is feeling what a person is feeling. You are there to comfort them and show you are there for them when they are in great mental pain and difficulty. Louise Evans, the founder of the *5 Chairs, 5 Choices* behavior concept, has created the following six-step process to help us connect with our empathy:

1. The best way to show empathy is to listen, not talk.
2. Begin by taking a deep breath, slowing down, and focusing on them; it's not about you.
3. Consciously recognize the opportunity you have to help a person in pain feel better by listening and showing your support. It's an excellent way to make a heartfelt, positive difference.
4. Open up all your channels of listening – ears, eyes, mind, body, and heart. If you do, the person you are trying to help and support will feel your genuine concern. In giving empathy, the feelings you express are far more important than your words.
5. Move into SILENT MODE. Just listen and nod, don't try to downplay it or share how you went through something similar. It's about them, not you.
6. Empathy is not about FIXING the person. This is counterproductive, and the antithesis of your purpose and their need.

"Empathy works so well because it does not require a solution. It requires only understanding." - John Medina

DO YOU ASPIRE TO INSPIRE OR
BE INSPIRED?

I t is the entrepreneur that forges the path and the leader that turns it into a highway. Entrepreneurial leaders can change our world - think Steve Jobs (Apple), Yvon Chouinard (Patagonia), Herb Kelleher (Southwest Airlines), Bill Gates (Microsoft), Reed Hastings (Netflix), Richard Branson (Virgin), Jeff Bezos (Amazon), and Elon Musk (Tesla). These legendary entrepreneurs not only changed our lives but altered the world as we know it.

Let's look at the difference between entrepreneurs and leaders. *Entrepreneurs are inspired.* They are visionaries and innovators. Bright shiny objects can lead to the next powerhouse idea and cause today's priorities to drop entirely off the radar. The critical measurement of their success is the impact of their ideas. Execution sometimes takes a back seat to innovation.

Leaders execute and realize they can't do it alone. *If you are a true leader, you inspire.* The leader measures success on the quality of their relationships and the process of turning the vision into reality.

Many entrepreneurs start their own businesses because they don't play well with others. They get an idea that bucks the system. It becomes a passion, and that passion takes the form of a business.

However, for that business to continue to grow and stay relevant, it takes leadership that inspires a myriad of diverse people - including customers, vendors, employees, investors, professional advisors, coaches, peers, and associates that require a human connection to manage them.

To be an inspired entrepreneur that learns how to inspire others is an extraordinary accomplishment.

THE 6 CS OF LEADERSHIP

As a result of doing seminars in communications skills with multiple business over 20 years, it dawned on me that that the most important characteristic of a leader can be summed up by the following '6 Cs':

- Competence
- Concern/Care
- Communication Skills
- Consistency
- Constructive Candor
- Connection

I further explain each of these characteristics below.

1. Competence

There can be no leaders without followers. If people believe you are incompetent, they are unlikely to follow you.

Leaders are:

- Visionaries

- Decisive
- Lifetime learners
- Relationship builders
- Able to identify, recognize, and recruit talent

Leaders:

- Lead by their ability to influence and motivate others
- Recognize they get the behavior they exhibit and tolerate
- Know how to delegate
- Are problem solvers and future-focused
- Earn the right to hold others to a higher standard

2. Concern/Care

"No one cares how much you know until they know how much you care." -
Theodore Roosevelt

Leaders:

- Have their team's backs
- Continually acknowledge and recognize talent and effort

3. Communication Skills

Leaders:

- Are pro-active listeners
- Are articulate
- Establish eye contact
- Recognize that the shortest distance between two points is clarity
- Become masters at paying attention
- Hear you
- Communicate to get it right the first time
- Ask questions

4. Consistency

Leaders:

- Stay on message.
- Make decisions that are aligned with their core values.
- Treat everyone fairly and don't show favorites
- Walk their talk
- Know that a strategy *du jour* is a recipe for disaster

5. Constructive Candor

Leaders:

- Understand that honesty without compassion is cruelty
- Make it their goal to challenge their teams to make them better
- Bring out the best in their team and hold them to a higher standard
- Praise in public and criticize in private

6. Connection

Leaders:

- Support their team and acknowledge contributions
- Foster that we are all in this together
- Are approachable
- Build great teams out of great individuals
- Believe in their teams (and their teams know it)
- Recognize that success is 1% strategy and 99% alignment

We hope that this is a valuable "check-in-list."

BUILT TO LAST

Several years ago, Eddie Mayfield, a former client and a friend interviewed me as his first guest on his radio show and shared with the audience that I'd given him the best business advice he'd ever received.

I sheepishly asked what I told him. Eddie said that he had decided to sell his business, and I had talked him out of it. He said, "I was making a nice living from Electronic Motor Drives and Automation (EMA) and was only working a few hours per week. I had great staff, including top-notch technicians and a superb general manager. The business was international, and my margins were enviable."

We crunched the numbers, looked at comparable sales of companies like his, and concluded that the market value of EMA was about three and a half times what Eddie was taking out every year. The business was growing, and it was unlikely a buyer would pay for its potential. That was about fifteen years ago. Since then, the company continues to grow every year, and Eddie says his job is to stay out of the way.

None of this would have happened if Eddie hadn't built a solid foundation, created a superb culture, and invested in hiring a diverse international team of skilled technicians.

At the root of EMA's business is the commitment to a core set of values that every employee must sign when hired and governs every aspect of how the company does business. These values not only reflect Eddie's Christian faith but also allow EMA's employees to be proud of what they do and where they do it. The values, along with a team of experienced and well-trained technicians and engineers, are what make EMA the leader in the industry as they complete their third decade. Their mantra is that "No One, ANYWHERE, is Better at Drives Than We Are!"

Employees are expected to embrace the following values:

- All persons are worthy of respect and courtesy, including employees, vendors, and customers.
- All people and businesses are treated fairly.
- We will be truthful.
- We will keep our word.
- Profanity and profane behavior are not allowed.
- We strive to deliver our services and products on time.
- We strive to do quality work.
- We stand behind our work.
- We charge a fair price for our work.

Eddie created a company that is built to last. For the first ten years, it was a mom-and-pop company with Eddie and Vicky Mayfield doing the right things. It has now grown into a highly respected and profitable professional company that has created a blueprint for other entrepreneurs to follow.

Eddie and Vicky's character and leadership skills cast a giant shadow.

- They have hired the right people and given them every reason to stay. They consistently attract the best possible attitudes and skills.
- The company is value-driven from top to bottom.
- They are committed to their customers.

- They give their best every day to each other and to their clients.
- They walk their talk and are the cutting-edge specialist in the drive industry.

Well done, Eddie and Vicky Mayfield.

HOW MANY EMOTIONS

BY GUEST CONTRIBUTOR, MAUREEN MCBRIDE RUSSAKOFF

As you may have gathered from previous posts, Rich and I are reading and studying *Atlas of The Heart* by Brené Brown. In her research for the book, she and her team surveyed 7,000 people over five years, and found, on average, people could identify only three emotions as they are feeling them: happiness, sadness, and anger.

Brené identified and categorized eighty-seven discrete emotional states to help people acquire or improve their emotional literacy.

Some of these states are listed below.

#1 Places we go When Things are Uncertain or Too Much

Stress, Overwhelmed, Anxiety, Worry, Avoidance, Excitement, Dread, Fear, Vulnerability

#8 Places we go When We Fall Short

Shame, Self-Compassion, Perfectionism, Guilt, Humiliation, Embarrassment

Recently in my coaching practice I carefully listened to four people, all working for the same company, who faced the same challenges.

They described those same challenges from the point of view of their personal feelings about the circumstances.

Each person was aware of and sympathetic to the stress their co-workers faced and would tell you they're good friends, yet none could turn to the other as allies.

A persistent underlying notion came through in the conversations; either they should accept blame, or their co-workers should.

Chapters twelve and thirteen of *Atlas of The Heart* covered some possible names for emotions that come up when you are caught in the blame game. Each one shared a deep concern and point of view, that the circumstances which were utterly out of their control, were in some way, underneath it all, evidence of their personal failings.

Stressful situations tend to trigger our worst perceptions of ourselves.

#12 Places we go When We Feel Wronged

Anger, Contempt, Distrust, Dehumanization, Hate, Self-Righteousness

#13 Places we go To Self-Assess

Pride, Hubris, Humility

My challenge, as I held diverse points of view that make up the bigger picture, was to encourage my clients to step into the beginner's mind. ("Shoshin" is a word from Zen Buddhism meaning "beginner's mind.")

This orientation of the mind refers to having an attitude of openness, eagerness, and a lack of preconceptions, just as a beginner would, and to ask oneself, "What would happen if no one were to blame?"

Objectively, it was abundantly clear to me that each person in this working quartet was trying their hardest to maintain a sense of status quo and equilibrium amidst a chaotic and unpredictable *phase*.

In this last sentence, the keyword, *"phase"* was what I shared with my clients. They were in a phase, and they had not given themselves permission to recognize this.

We're going through changes, and this, too, shall pass. There will be a new normal, and we will have something less akin to quicksand under our feet soon. Harmony will return. The real question remains: What will we have learned?

KINTSUGI POTTERY

*"Never be afraid about being broken
because strength is nothing but pain that's been repaired."* - Trent Shelton

M oe recently introduced me to Kintsugi pottery and what do you know! It came up in a conversation I had the following day with Joe Hickey, sales manager of Lekker Furniture and an enthusiastic potter. We talked about this most beautiful Japanese art form, which led me to do a little more research and meditate on the concept.

Kintsugi is the Japanese art of putting broken pottery pieces back together with gold. It is built on the idea that when you embrace flaws and imperfections, you can create stronger and even more beautiful pieces of art.

The philosophy behind Kintsugi is to value an object's beauty, as well as its imperfections, giving them equal attention as something to celebrate, not disguise.

Using this as a metaphor for healing ourselves teaches an important lesson: Sometimes, in the process of repairing things that have broken, we create something more unique, beautiful, and resilient.

In her new book, *Kintsugi Wellness: The Japanese Art of Nourishing Mind, Body, and Spirit*, Candice Kumai explores the powerful message behind Kintsugi. She writes, "Whether you're going through the loss of a loved one or a job, or are recovering from an injury, divorce or personal tragedy, Kintsugi can be a way to reframe hardships."

Please remind yourself that you are not a victim of your circumstances — and you can come out on the other side stronger.

"You won't realize your full potential until you go through the tough times," Kumai says.

"Wellness is about the practice of resilience, overcoming challenges, and being a better version of yourself with all of your golden cracks."

"When the storm rips you to pieces, you get to decide how to put yourself back together." - Bryant McGill.

FOUR PERSONALITY STYLES

R ecently Moe and I were on a call with a company's COO who struggled to communicate effectively with another team member. It was only after we finished the call that I realized what one of their challenges may have been. Their personality styles clashed. The COO had an Analytical personality style, making decisions slowly and requiring the time necessary to think through all of the potential options. It's a systematic approach. It's "Ready, set, go" in slow motion. The other leadership team member had a Driver personality style, had little patience, and wanted to just get the job done. This personality style is a fast "Go, go, go" approach.

Identifying and understanding personality styles makes you a better communicator and salesperson. While both the Analytical and Driver personality styles are task-oriented, the person with the Analytical style strives to avoid emotional conflict, while the Driver will challenge you to focus on results rather than the process. Neither fall victim to wanting to be loved like the Amiable and the Expressive styles.

If you understand your personality style and others you are working with, you can skillfully get in their box and make them feel comfortable. The Amiable speaks and makes decisions slowly. They want to avoid conflict and make everyone happy. They are the team's diplomats. The Expressive pays little attention to details, and like the Driver, moves fast to get the job done.

If you are selling to a:

- **Driver** - Don't give them your opinion (they don't want it). Just give them the facts, answer the questions they ask, and they will tell you what they want.
- **Analytical** - Know that they want data and then more information before making a decision. They have analysis paralysis and the fear of making the wrong decision. Once the Analytical determines they have all the information needed, only then will they pull the trigger.
- **Amiable** - Remember that they are buying you. They want to know about your family and how old your kids are. They want to trust you. They will move slowly and will seek out your opinion and assurances as part of their decision-making process.
- **Expressive** - Don't bore them with the details. They are buying the "big dream", they think fast and act faster. They also tend to be charismatic and good leaders.

What I've shared in this post is the right amount of information for the Expressive and the Driver. It's high level, told quickly, not bogged down with details, and cuts to the chase.

There are countless books on the four personality styles for lifetime learners and the curious if you wish to learn more about them.

YOU GET MORE OF THE
BEHAVIOR YOU REWARD

"The primary purpose of a business is to achieve results. The focus of leaders and managers must be to reward the results you want." - Ichak Adizes

Too many managers and business owners fall into the trap of playing a "cop" as "the best way" to eliminate unproductive or even counterproductive behavior. The principle of positive reinforcement makes coaching work best, and it is the reason you get more of the behaviors you reward.

I found it is much more effective to be a coach than a cop. The best way to accomplish this is to identify and reward the behaviors you want, and to encourage your team to aspire to higher performance levels. As a coach, you want to "catch 'em doing something right" and let them know how much you appreciate their excellent work.

Psychologists teach that immediate positive reinforcement is the most reliable method of achieving and maintaining positive performance. Punishment (most often anger) breeds paranoia and poor morale. Negative reinforcement and lack of attention to either good or bad performance tell employees that there is a low value placed on them and their efforts.

As coaches, leaders, managers, teachers, or parents, our focus must be clear regarding the results we want and the actions that produce them.

Desirable behavior is too precious to take for granted. Please touch someone with love today; it is life's most splendid gift.

ROCKS AND SWOTS

I encourage the companies I coach to embrace the concept of creating quarterly and annual rocks. To get there we start with a SWOT Analysis. I'd like to share with you what a "rock" is and what SWOT Analysis is and show you how and why to make them a part of establishing and initiating priorities.

Rocks are the most important things that must get done. What distinguishes a "rock" from other initiatives is that a rock is a strategic objective that will move the company's needle.

Ideally, every quarter you will focus on three to four rocks. Completing them will make a significant difference in productivity, customer relations, internal systems, and processes, competing in the marketplace, enhancing strengths, minimizing weaknesses, and making sure we don't fall victim to threats.

We all have activities that we do on a day-to-day basis. As Stephen Covey wrote in *The 7 Habits of Highly Effective People*, we spend most of our productive time on *"important and urgent activities."* It does not leave us time for initiatives that are the most critical to a company's growth.

The best way to determine a "rock" is to ask each member of your leadership team to participate in a SWOT analysis exercise.

SWOT is an acronym for Strengths, Weaknesses, Opportunities, and Threats.

STRENGTHS

Your strengths and your weaknesses are a snapshot of where the company is today. A list of a company's strengths might be:

- The knowledge of how to leverage a company's competitive advantage for a larger market share
- Recruitment
- Introduction of new products or services
- Retention of clients
- Loyal customers

WEAKNESSES

Considerations for weakness can include:

- Cashflow
- New competition
- Turnover of key personnel
- Systems and processes that are unscalable
- A lack of alignment or clear direction

OPPORTUNITIES

Responding to the market is a huge competitive advantage. Here are some examples:

- Trends in the marketplace
- A strategic relationship
- Growth through social media, potential new clients
- Buying out a competitor

THREATS

Proactively dealing with threats is critical, such as:

- New legislation
- Covid-19
- Price Wars
- Shrinking margins
- Loss of major clients

To complete your SWOT analysis, the company must identify which three or four rocks you should focus on within the next quarter. Then create the rock or initiative for each that will have the most impact on the company.

It's critically important for one person to:

- Own the rock.
- Clearly define the rock.
- Determine who should assist, including internal and external resources.
- Create a budget and timelines for milestones.
- Create a Plan B because sometimes things don't work out the way you think they will.
- Articulate what will be the benefit to the company by completing the rock.

Your rocks enable you to take giant steps forward instead of just focusing on the day-to-day things that consume most of your time.

Rock on, brothers and sisters.

THE GREATEST OPPORTUNITIES
ARE WITHIN

"What lies behind us and what lies before us are tiny matters compared with what lies within us." - Oliver Wendell Holmes

The greatest opportunities are within your imagination and self-awareness.

Opportunities are created by weaving new combinations out of old ideas.

Imagination is the mirror of the soul. Your imagination belongs to you. The more you use it, the more efficiently it will serve you. Imagination is the workshop of the human mind, where old ideas and facts may be reassembled into new combinations and put to new uses. There is nothing new under the sun. HOWEVER, there IS imagination.

Thoughts + Imagination = The workshop of the soul.

Be yourself, your authentic self. Change requires breaking patterns. Interrupt a way you do something enough times, and it will change. Hold yourself to a higher standard. The same level of thinking that got you where you are won't get you to the next level.

"In developing our self-awareness, many of us discover ineffective scripts, deeply embedded habits that are unworthy of us, and incongruent with the things we value. However, once we tap into our self-awareness, we must realize that we are responsible for using our imagination and creativity to write new scripts congruent with our deepest values." - Dr. Stephen Covey

The Anwar Sadat Transition

When Sadat became President of Egypt and confronted the political realities, he rescripted himself toward Israel. He visited the Knesset in Jerusalem and opened up one of the most precedent-breaking peace movements in the history of the world. This bold initiative eventually brought about the Camp David accords. His change began while he was in prison.

"I found that I faced a highly complex situation and couldn't hope to change it until I had armed myself with the necessary psychological and intellectual capacity. My contemplation of life and human nature in that secluded place (Cell 54) has taught me that he who cannot change the very fabric of his thought will never be able to change reality and will never, therefore, make any progress." - Anwar Sadat

To fully realize our opportunities that lie within:

- Tap into your imagination.
- Take your game to a higher level.
- Hold yourself to a higher standard.
- Take a reflective look at yourself and be willing to change the very fabric of your thoughts.

Imagination plus self-awareness is the path to finding the most incredible opportunities lying within you.

"Imagination is more important than knowledge for knowledge is limited, whereas imagination embraces the entire world, stimulating progress, and giving birth to evolution." - Albert Einstein

TO A MAN WITH A HAMMER
EVERYTHING LOOKS LIKE A NAIL

"To a man with a hammer, everything looks like a nail." - Abraham Maslow.

Recently I was on a call with an entrepreneur and former athlete who shared that the best way to motivate him was a firm kick in the butt, so that is his approach to motivate others.

For some, that is the ideal approach. For others, it can result in resentment, depression, or cause them to shut down or even quit.

The legendary football coach Jimmy Johnson said about coaching, "there is nothing so unequal as the equal treatment of unequal." This means what motivates one will not motivate all. Humans respond to different approaches, and the more we internalize that, the more success we will have in our lives.

Great leaders, motivators, and salespeople either know instinctively or have learned over time that the best way to motivate people is to meet them in their comfort zone. Knowing how to motivate someone is an art that can be learned with practice and paying attention.

I like to say as a business coach; I am the CEO's CEO or Chief Encouragement Officer.

While most people respond to encouragement, the more we understand what motivates an individual, the more likely we create win-win results.

If we pay attention, people will teach us how to motivate them. Look for the signs; they are there.

Some respond best to:

- Being given a challenge.
- Not wanting to let us down.
- Receiving constant hand holding
- Ongoing direction.
- Telling them what you want and getting out of their way
- Being thanked in advance
- A sense of responsibility
- The desire to exceed expectations
- The opportunity to grow
- The recognition that there will be negative consequences if they fail.
- Knowing there will be a positive reward or a bonus if they succeed.

Rachel Weisberg, our fantastic Communications Director and frequent contributor to Food for Thought, shared a story about how a nurse motivated her to keep pushing while she was delivering her baby. The date was March 16, and Rachel's husband's name is Michael Kelly. Rachel had mentioned to the nurse that she did not want their baby with the last name of Kelly to be born on Saint Patrick's Day.

Rachel said that every time she wanted to rest and wait, the nurse reminded her that if she waited, her baby would be born on St. Patrick's Day, and the clock was ticking. That motivation was what it took for their baby to be celebrating her second birthday next Wednesday, March 16.

I believe Rachel's nurse has learned through 100's deliveries to listen for clues from her patients on motivating them through the delivery process.

Like Rachel's nurse, those who have mastered the art of motivating others are keen observers, excellent listeners, build trust and demonstrate to others that they care about them.

"The only thing worse than a coach or CEO who doesn't care about their people are ones who pretend to care. People can spot a phony every time." - Jimmy Johnson

A RETURN TO CREATIVE MARKETING

M any years ago on a visit to Las Vegas, the cab driver who drove me from the airport to my hotel, told me not to miss the Kenny Rogers show while I was in town. He went on to say that Rogers does a free concert for cab drivers, concierges, and waitstaff during his final dress rehearsal.

Moe shared with me that she didn't want to sing to empty seats when she had residencies at nightclubs in Chicago. She believed it was her job to fill the seats, so she paid a visit to every hotel on Michigan Avenue to invite the concierge. She offered them two complimentary tickets and drinks for her show. It worked. The seats were always full. She made her real money selling her signed CDs after each performance.

During my career, I've always considered speaking gigs as paid marketing. Whenever we speak at a conference or facilitate a retreat, we always stay for the entire event and participate in activities. It's where the magic happens, and you have the opportunity to connect one on one.

At the High Point Furniture Show in North Carolina, I would walk around and talk to the owners at their booths. I shared with them that

I coach clients in the furniture industry. This is how I generated business.

At R&R Junction, my first business on the Outer Banks of North Carolina, we held two wine and cheese parties for the waitstaff at all the local restaurants every spring. Who better to recommend us to the tourist trade?

It is important to be creative and schedule events to network and promote business. Nothing beats face-to-face marketing. If you approach it by asking current clients or prospects what their goals and challenges are and how you can serve them better, you may end up with more business than any sales call. It works best if you ask questions and listen. Once prospects open up and share with you their opportunities and challenges, you are halfway home.

One of our clients plans an annual 4th Quarter west coast tour to meet with clients. He intended to listen, learn and introduce a new product designed to provide a solution to meet the needs of the industry.

When the timing is right, how can your business benefit from face-to-face meetings? How can your business benefit from the method Moe used, sell and tell by walking around and meeting the very people who can become your fans and in turn, send you customers?

ASK YOUR CLIENTS

A client recently asked me and his CEO to determine what their company's unique competitive advantage should be. I suggested we ask their clients.

One of the most crucial roles of the CEO is receiving feedback from clients to learn what they are doing right, what they can do better, and to look for future opportunities.

In a recent conversation with another client, he said he intended to dedicate considerable time to visiting his customers in the future after the COVID pandemic subsides.

He recently learned that many clients and prospective clients requested his company to provide an additional offering. They requested for his service providers to perform the initial setup to activate their company's proprietary software program. This service will allow prospective clients to say 'yes' faster and onboard quicker. He also learned that many clients want to outsource the entire implementation and maintenance to the company.

My client discovered this by making the effort to meet his customers face to face. My client's company lacks the capacity to offer the service today but plans to implement it in the future. This will now become an additional profit center, client pleaser, and make their software stickier.

Stew Leonards is a world-famous grocery store chain founded in Connecticut. They are also famous for the focus groups they hold with their customers. In one focus group, customers shared their wish that Leonards carried fresh fish instead of their present offerings of fish stored in Styrofoam containers. Leonards was surprised because their fish was purchased every morning from New York's Fulton Fish Market, so it could not be fresher. They learned their customers wanted fish sold on ice, giving it the perception of being just caught. Subsequently, Leonards now offers fish both ways, and the sales for fish have doubled.

Customers also expressed their preference for buying strawberries loose instead of in containers. This is because, in the containers, there are always one or two rotten strawberries. They wanted to make their own selection. When Stew Leonards offered strawberries loose, the average purchase nearly doubled.

When I worked with INC Magazine, I was a frequent speaker at their conferences. I asked Linda Burton, the conference coordinator, why I was repeatedly asked to speak? I expected her to say it was because of my content or high ratings. Instead, she said that so many speakers are primadonnas. "You are easy to work with, and that makes my job easier."

When I ask my clients what they value most about our coaching relationship, they tell me I am an excellent sounding board.

Whenever someone is considering hiring me for a speaking engagement, I tell them that I am easy to work with and then prove it. I also make sure I am there for my clients whenever they need a sounding board.

Asking your clients or customers for feedback may be the highest and best use of a CEO's time. If you don't believe me, ask your clients.

JUST SAY NO

"NO to distractions is a YES to focus and space for creativity." - Tanmay Vora

When we say YES to always being available to the world, we say NO to focus.

How do we think, plan, execute, review, and accomplish if we do not focus on what's important to us?

It's easy to get caught up in what Steven Covey called quadrant three activities - urgent, but unimportant tasks. These can include activities like spending the day responding to emails, calls, and time-consuming errands. Your days fly by, but nothing of value gets done.

Saying no and delegating is hard, so we tend to tell ourselves:

- It is easier just to do it than to delegate
- Somebody's gotta do it
- Their project is more important than mine
- I like being needed

We can spend our entire lives serving others and not ourselves and our goals. A dream is a goal without a deadline.

In Louise Evans' "Five Chairs, Five Choices" TEDx speech, she talks about the importance of asking "What do I want?" That is the vital question to ask to clarify what is important to you. In Louise Evans's "Five Chairs, Five Choices" TEDx video, she says;

"Once you have identified what YOU want, give yourself permission and the necessary time to make it happen. Don't play the martyr or the victim. We are better than that, and we all deserve to live the life that matters to us. If we do not focus on what we want, no one else will."

In the words of the scholar Hillel, written in the first century CE from the Talmud:

"If I am not for myself, then who is for me, but if I am for myself alone, then what am I? And if not now, when?" - Hillel

A DIFFERENT POINT OF VIEW

"Most great people have attained their greatest success just one step beyond their greatest failure." - Napoleon Hill

In my view, the most impressive player on the field during the 2021 Super Bowl (for the 2020 season) was Patrick Mahomes. Yes, by the numbers, it was his worst performance as a pro, and yes, he did not throw a touchdown for the entire game.

Let's look at what he did well. I found it so impressive how he dodged tacklers, changed directions, and found a way to throw passes consistently just before being tackled or hit. It takes extraordinary talent to keep a play alive facing the Tampa Bay Buccaneers rushers.

The best quarterback and receivers create plays that depend on split-second timing and spacing. Neither Mahomes nor his receivers had that luxury on Sunday. Many of Mahomes' throws could have been caught, but the Buccaneers' defense had the entire Chief offense out of its flow.

Over the past months, the team lost three all-pro members of their offensive line for the season due to injuries. The tenacious Tampa Bay

Buccaneers defensive line made Swiss cheese out of the patchwork replacements for the Chiefs.

Had Brady or almost any other great quarterback faced similar circumstances, they would likely have suffered the same fate. Throughout it all, Mahomes kept his poise and never gave up.

Brady deservedly to win the MVP, but it was the Buccaneers' relentless defensive line and defensive backs that iced Tampa Bay's victory. It was their extraordinary team effort on both sides of the ball.

Pat and the Chiefs will be back. They are a terrific team which not only dealt with irreplaceable losses on the field, but they also had to deal with the tragedy of Head Coach Andy Reid's son, Britt Reid, who was the Chiefs outside linebackers' coach, being involved in a three-car crash on Thursday night in Kansas City.

He did not travel with the Chiefs to Tampa, Florida, for the Super Bowl. Britt Reid acknowledged to police that he was driving the vehicle that collided with two other cars, including the one with a 5-year-old girl fighting for her life.

The best leaders, coaches, managers, teachers, and parents have the vision to catch people demonstrating courage and leadership while managing their emotions in the worst of circumstances. Under these circumstances, Mahomes shined.

Every competitor faces losses and disappointments throughout their career. Patrick Mahomes, who was awarded Super Bowl MVP in 2020, showed as much courage and character in defeat in 2021 as he did in victory the previous year.

"Success is not final; failure is not fatal. It is the courage to continue that counts." - Winston Churchill

Make today the day you recognize the success in your failures and carry on.

FINDING YOUR ZONE OF GENIUS
IN THE WORKPLACE

I n his book *Big Leap*, Gay Hendricks describes the concept of four different 'zones' that someone can be in depending on where their strengths, talent and skills lie.

As explained below, these zones range from 'Zone of Incompetence' to 'Zone of Genius', with each zone describing how the person feels when doing a task and how proficient they will be at completing it. It can be useful to consider these zones when delegating work and defining an employee's roles and responsibilities.

Task Description - Zone of Employee Doing the Task

- Activities they suck at - Zone of Incompetence
- Activities they are okay at, but don't excel in - Zone of Competence
- Activities they are good at but others are better - Zone of Excellence "Trap"*
- Activities they are excited about and do exceptionally well - Zone of Genius

Why "trap?" Because while the employee may be good at these activities, they don't light us up and they make people feel stuck.

We discovered many people wore too many hats and while they did some activities in their Zone of Genius, they performed too many other tasks in their Zones of Incompetence or Competence.

But, if you redistribute tasks according to what is in each individual's Zone of Genius, and remove tasks they do not do so well, it would be obvious to see how each person would perform at their highest level. Thereby, the company could accomplish more.

The opportunity to recast a company is exciting; not by fixing the past but by creating the future. When people are working in their Zones of Genius and are on the right seat on the bus, they can move mountains.

The next step is to look at these roles and responsibilities and decide who should do what and where. This involves exploring how an individual's tasks can be reconsidered so that everyone is performing at their best each day; loving what they do and contributing to success.

Finally, there is a difference between self-confidence and self-compassion. I asked a group to share what they thought is more important to a person's success: self-confidence or self-compassion? They were split 50/50.

My answer is that self-compassion is the key. Nobody's perfect. Give yourself a break. Don't feel like you have to be perfect to do things right. And don't beat yourself up. Learn and move on. Give yourself the benefit of the doubt.

LIFE TAKEAWAYS FROM "TAKING YOUR BIG LEAP WITH RICH RUSSAKOFF"

❦

BY GUEST CONTRIBUTOR RACHEL WEISBERG

I 've been on the edge of a "life cliff", scrambling to keep my toes from slipping off, for years now.

I have good intentions, (arguably) great ideas, lots of skills, a positive spirit, and warm energy. What I don't have is passion and my own personal secret sauce to get my life moving in the right direction.

Enter Rich's workshop - Taking Your Big Leap - which I attended in the Spring of 2021. In this intimate workshop filled with some real gems, I learned the following:

- "It's" already in me.
- All I need to do is identify the things I'm really great at (not good - *GREAT*), things that bring me joy, that light my fire, and that make me smile. That's my Zone of Genius. These are the things that I have mastered and do better than everyone else.
- When I stay in that Zone of Genius, I will live a happy, fulfilling life with fewer barriers and more lightness.

Easy, right?

Well, no. It's not. For a number of reasons:

1. I am *pretty good* at a lot of things - this is my *Zone of Excellence*. I'm borderline great even, BUT not overjoyed. Satisfied *but not lit up*. It's MUCH SIMPLER to exist in that Zone of Excellence because I'm excellent but not truly stretched and/or challenged.
2. *Because my brain gets in the way*, I'm full of self-doubt. I'm certain that I'm fundamentally flawed (an Upper Limit Barrier). I get in my own way.

As Rich says, *"Don't believe everything you think."* Your thoughts are powerful. If you settle into negative self-talk, your brain starts to change. Your brain will mold to those thoughts. Think good thoughts!

A day after attending the workshop, I got a haircut. My hairstylist and I were chatting about life in general (as we do). I mentioned that since I'm working WAY less, *I feel like I should be fit, and the house should be spotless.* She said to me: "My therapist always says *don't should on your-self,*" and oh my, did that resonate!

The pun is great, but to show yourself true compassion, to really take a step back and be kind to ALL of you, requires not "living in shoulds." It requires not believing all the things you think, especially if those thoughts are laced with doubt.

As Rich teaches, it requires relying more on self-compassion and TRUST.

Self-compassion is giving myself permission to work in MY flow; to ignore the "shoulds" and identify the things that make me tick. I can fuel my self-love by identifying the ways that I'm unique, talented, and gifted. Self-compassion is deeper than self-confidence. It is acceptance, love, and patience all rolled into a neat package and tied with a bow.

What sets this program apart from other workshops on similar topics I've attended, was the intimate, personal experience of sharing MY

Zones, Upper Limit Barriers, and self with the other attendees. I'll keep the detail to a minimum to protect their privacy but learning what made the others tick really enriched the experience. We all came away feeling more connected, more compassionate, and clearer on how to create a Life Worth Living and, as Rich would say, how to live "in the zone."

YOUR TEAM IS YOUR MOST
IMPORTANT STAKEHOLDER

"Before the pandemic, customers were considered the most important business stakeholders. Now, it's employees." - Mike Allen-Axios

A business is only as good as its people. Every entrepreneur is in the hiring, requiring, inspiring, firing, communications, and training business. The retention of great people is every company's top-tier Key Performance Indicator (KPI).

As previously mentioned, my mantra has always been to "hire the best and fire the pests." Jim Collins, author of *Good to Great*, writes that "great people" are three times more productive than "good people." People with talent, dedication, imagination, self-pride, who work well with others, and who have a can-do attitude will always find opportunities in the marketplace. The leader and management's job is to give these ideal employees appropriate responsibility and let them know how much they value and appreciate them.

A year after the pandemic, people are reassessing:

- Their career paths
- Their priorities
- The time they want to spend with family

- The lost time spent commuting daily
- Their benefits, especially healthcare
- Their future opportunities

Now is the time for leaders and managers to have one-on-one conversations with key talent and ask them:

- What are your goals and aspirations?
- How can we make your career with the company the best possible experience?
- What do you like best about working at the company?
- What do you like least?
- If you had three wishes for the company, what would they be?
- What do you like best about your job?
- What do you like least about your job?
- What can we do to make this the best company to work for?
- What ideas do you have to improve the company?

Listen well and show you care. Share with everyone the company's goals and the future opportunities that are possible.

It is also an excellent time to recruit talent who have decided to change their job or career path. Can-do people are seeking new opportunities. Now is the time to harvest, and don't be afraid to pay people what they are worth within your budget.

Focus on keeping the talent you have and recruiting the best people to continue to grow. And if you are in the workplace looking for a better path, now is the time to search for the right job with the right company. You deserve nothing less.

FINDING GREAT TALENT

The best recruiting grounds may be where you go for coffee or dine out. Many years ago, Four Hands was looking for a good customer service representative, with no success. While working with them for one week in Austin, Texas, I was staying near a coffee and breakfast shop where I had breakfast each morning. The first morning my server wore a flower in her hair. I complimented her on it. Her service was terrific, and we talked about her goals and aspirations.

The second morning, I told her about Four Hands and asked her if she would like to meet the Four Hands CEO, Brett Hatton, to discuss the position in their Customer Service department.

The following day Brett Hatton met me for breakfast at the coffee shop, and I introduced them to each other. By Monday, she was on board. She was a quick learner and a breath of fresh air for the department. Within the next three months, she recruited two other superstars for us.

Recently Moe and I had dinner at a four-star Italian restaurant on Federal Hill in Providence, Rhode Island. Our waitress was upbeat, warm, articulate, fully present, and paid attention to details. I asked her name, and she said it was Bennie, which is short for Benedetta Viti. She came to the United States from Italy when she was 14 years old.

I asked her to recommend a wine. She asked what characteristics I was looking for, and her choice was excellent. Later, we were selecting dessert and I asked if the chocolate was a good choice. Without hesitation, she said yes, but the salted caramel was the best in the house and to die for.

Moe was impressed that she was not afraid to assert herself and asked Bennie if she was in college. Bennie said she was and majored in Marketing. Moe followed with a further inquiry about her curriculum and if it included an internship. Bennie said she would need an internship. Moe told her about the nature of our business and asked if she is interested. She said she was and gave us her email address to schedule an interview. We emailed her and she immediately responded, providing several alternative times she would be available.

Everything she did in setting up the interview was what she would need to do on the job:

- She was on time
- She dressed professionally
- She communicated well about the setup for the meeting
- She was flexible on times she could be available
- She told Moe it was an exciting opportunity, and she was grateful to be considered.

Moe and Lucy, our marketing director, interviewed Bennie. After the call, Lucy said to Moe, "Well, it looks like you found another exceptional candidate." When we interface with people, we always look for the qualities of the character we want to hire.

People who:

- Are upbeat
- Pay attention to detail

- Have presence and are present
- Have emotional intelligence
- Are articulate
- Are warm
- Are people-oriented
- Are confident

Finding great talent begins with recognizing and proactively looking for the qualities you want and never missing an opportunity to hire the best.

HAPPY HUNTING. THE TALENT YOU ARE SEEKING IS LOOKING FOR YOU

BY GUEST CONTRIBUTOR MAUREEN MCBRIDE

I f you struggle to find the talent you need in a tight labor market, I strongly urge you to consider working with a distributed, sometimes called 'remote' or 'virtual' team.

Throughout the ups and downs of almost two years of this pandemic, Coach to the Best has recruited and worked with a team that has over time included talent from Ireland, France, India, the Philippines, Austin, TX, Baltimore MD, Philadelphia, PA, and most recently, Providence RI.

To fill in the gaps between skills and the needs of our business enterprises, we offer project-based work to contractors using Upwork.

The more laser-focused your description of the tasks you are hiring for is, the more successful you will be at attracting a perfect fit for the job and your company culture.

The contract workers on Upwork tend to be more entrepreneurial and guard their ratings zealously. Contract money is held in escrow accounts and dispersed once a week for ongoing agreements or held until the contract is complete to the satisfaction of the hiring party.

What about trust? Start with trusting yourself to know what you want, learn how to explain it, and have a good idea in your mind of how long it should take to complete the project. You can include all of these elements in your agreement with the contract worker.

Below is a sample of an ad that we ran when we were looking for talent:

International Company Seeks "A" Player

An extremely rare opportunity for a person with an entrepreneurial "whatever it takes" attitude.

Seeking an infinitely curious support person who loves variety and is invested in personal growth.

You will work in tandem with an international team of professional business advisors to co-create funding packages for businesses to grow, even in a shrinking economic climate. Your work will NOT focus on numbers, spreadsheets, etc.--you will be working on the marketing narrative side of the funding packages with two bonafide O.G. Superstars.

Your positive, can-do attitude is much more important than the details of your resume or education.

You will need stellar English writing and editing skills and the ability to take direction as well as take the initiative. When you come to us with a challenge, you also can recommend a solution.

Happy hunting. Remember, the talent you are seeking is looking for you.

THE WONDER QUESTION

∞

"Our doubts are traitors that cause us to lose the good we might achieve by failing the attempt." - William Shakespeare

Last year, I had the opportunity to interview a dear friend, Louise Evans. Louise is the author of *5 Chairs, 5 Choices,* and I recommend this book to everyone. You won't find a better book on emotional intelligence. It is well written and researched. I have underlined insights from every page in the book. In addition, her TEDx talk on the 5 Chairs concept, entitled "Own Your Behaviors, Master Your Communication, Determine Your Success" has received over 4.7 million hits on YouTube.

Our conversation took us to the importance of assessing a situation based upon objective facts, before attempting to correct another's behavior. Louise shared with me how fear plays a fundamental role in our inability to exercise our leadership and management responsibilities in holding others accountable.

I shared with Louise a conversation I had with the newly appointed COO of a client, an eyelash extension salon, I was working with. I asked her for her recommendation on how best I can handle it.

The COO wrote me the following message:

"Hi Rich! I'm currently at our location and have an opportunity to correct a team member that is out of our dress code. She is currently wearing a hat backward when our policy allows for hats, but only on Monday[s] and not backward. This is what I have drafted, any feedback?

'Hello! While I love your personal style, I'd like to remind you of our dress code/hat policy. Our mission is to create the ultimate lash experience - and our dress code is in place to help establish that image! Please be sure to only wear hats on Mondays and not backward! Thank you so much for your understanding!'"

It sounded good to me, yet I knew something was missing.

Louise suggested that the COO start with a **"wonder question."** I wonder why you chose to wear the hat backward. Then listen for the answer and, depending on what she says, say something like "I see that you wanted to express your individuality, and that's great outside of work. We are working as a team at the salon, so please stay consistent with the image we have created."

The question takes the judgment out of the conversation and allows the other person to share their reasons. This approach will enable you to focus on the negative behavior and not the person. It also requests the worker to be part of the team look. After the interview with Louise, I called the COO and the CEO immediately and shared Louise's wisdom.

Many managers never address issues with employees for fear that it will lead to defensiveness and counterproductivity. Therefore, they keep it to themselves, then fall into the trap of "toxic silence" by not addressing the problem at all. It's a lose-lose approach.

By asking the wonder question and focusing on the behavior, you can change the dynamic, eliminate defensiveness, not stew in toxic silence, and correct the behavior.

When the opportunity presents itself, ask the "I wonder" question, and begin with curiosity, NOT JUDGEMENT.

THREE FINANCIAL DOCUMENTS EVERY ENTREPRENEUR MUST MASTER

⚜

O vercome the fear of financial statements and understand how to read these documents. This is every entrepreneur's responsibility. It begins with demanding real-time, easy-to-understand financial information. And remember that if you control your money, you control your future.

Every entrepreneur must understand the following three reports:

1. **Accounts Receivable Aging Report**

Accurate accounts receivable aging reports will:

- Be the basis for projecting future revenue that you will need to pay your bills
- Highlight any customers that are is late paying you for your products or services
- Be the basis for establishing a line of credit with a bank. Most banks will lend you up to 80% on receivables under 90 days
- Let you know if your collections department is effective at collecting debts due on a timely basis

2. **Profit and Loss (P&L) Statement**

Break down your revenue and cost of goods by profit centers, so you know what profit centers are your cash cows, and what are your sick puppies. This gives great insight into what profit centers are making you money and which ones are costing you money. You might be surprised. **Put your money where the most significant return is.**

Prevent margin creep costs. If your profit and loss statements break down each item's percentages of total revenue, you will understand your margins and spot margin trends. Margin creep occurs when expenses like materials, health care, insurance, utilities, wages, and rent increase. Any company importing goods from China today has been hit by increased shipping costs and the renting facilities in ports exploding.

I helped a client break down their cost as 60% all-in for labor, 10% for marketing, 20% for sales, general, and administrative expenses (SG&A) giving them a bottom-line profit of 10%. So, if labor costs rise four more points, marketing two points, and SG&A goes up by 5%, the company is in the red.

Also, remember to categorize expenses by category and not alphabetically.

When I see a P&L where the first expense is accounting, the second is advertising, and the third is auto, I know someone is using a QuickBooks template, and they have no idea what their expenses are by category.

3. **Balance Sheet**

The final document that you must become a master of is the Balance Sheet. Unfortunately, most entrepreneurs have not learned the value of an accurate balance sheet and don't know how to read it.

Yet, the balance sheet is the first document a banker wants to see and the best way for you to keep score. Why? Because a banker wants to see that your short-term assets are double your short-term liabilities. A great KPI for any company comes straight from the balance sheet -

it's your current cash over your current liabilities (the "current ratio"). Ideally, you want it to be at least two to one.

Having a ratio of at least 2:1 shows that you have enough resources in the business to cover your day-to-day debts as they fall due. This is a measure of liquidity and helps us understand the financial health of the company.

Short-term assets include cash on hand and receivables under 90 days, and short-term liabilities include accounts payable and debt service you must pay within the current year. If this is over your head, you need to do some homework.

The balance sheet tells you if you are growing in assets or shrinking, and you can compare it by month, against last year's numbers, or against other competitors in the industry as a benchmark. It's how savvy entrepreneurs keep score.

All three documents taken together will enable you to understand your current financial picture and will highlight if you could have potential cash shortages over the next few months.

GUARANTEED TO DECREASE MORALE AND REDUCE PRODUCTIVITY

BY GUEST CONTRIBUTOR MAUREEN MCBRIDE

R ecently a random tweet caught my attention:

> *"Millennials and micromanagement do not mix."*

I dashed off a reply: *"Micromanagement is not management, it's an obsession disguised as a concern."*

As they say, it "blew up." People were responding and retweeting that sentence for days with the consensus point of view: Micromanagement is all about needing control. The idea that micromanagement demonstrates a lack of trust came up repeatedly. Unsurprisingly, no pro-micromanagement opinions were offered. Nada. Zip. Zilch. No one replied with the idea, "Oh yes! I love being micromanaged."

According to a survey released by the Robert Half staffing agency, 6 out of 10 Americans reported they'd experienced micromanagement at some point throughout their careers. What's more, 68% said it decreased their morale, and 55% said it hurt their productivity.

If you feel tempted to micromanage, ask yourself if your goal is to decrease morale and reduce productivity. If not, take a deep breath and remember micromanagement is a reflection of the anxiety the manager is feeling. A more helpful way to set aside fears and anxiety is to work on your communication and delegation skills.

Are you and the person you are managing in a relaxed and focused state when defining the tasks and planning the steps for execution? Do you have clear agreements on timelines and benchmarks? Are you communicating, preferably in a daily huddle/check-in meeting? And last but never least, are you consistently acknowledging and rewarding the behaviors and performance you want and need from your staff?

Rich's motto is "Delegate, but don't abdicate." His work style is highly collaborative; mine is highly independent. Subsequently, my motto is more like: "Either execute or delegate, but don't try both."

A TALE OF TWO DEPARTURES

"Your Spirit Shows in Everything You Do" - Philip Toshio Sudo

In the past few months, the COOs of two of my clients announced they were taking positions with other companies.

I had the opportunity to talk to both before they made their decision. It was the right choice for them. One was burnt out and needed a change. The other loved the job and the company, but the offer he was considering was too good to turn down.

The burnt-out COO gave one-week notice. She left just as a major initiative was about to begin and, in doing so, left the company in the lurch.

The other gave his company a month's notice and worked diligently every day to ensure that the CEO and his replacement were up to speed on their systems and processes. He also made sure there was a smooth transition with their clients and team members.

Both companies are terrific to work for, and they understand that they are always at risk of losing a good person. It goes with the territory. They understood and encouraged the COOs to make the best decision for them.

I believe in the importance of taking the long view and leaving professional relationships on a high note. It is a small world, and your reputation goes with you throughout your life.

Ask yourself, how do you want to be remembered? All the good you have achieved and the excellent work you've done can be tarnished by how you choose to leave.

When leaving a position, if it's in your control, exit with dignity and grace. It may not always be easy, but if you go out with class, you'll never regret it.

HIRING WITHOUT REQUIRING IS
A SETUP FOR FAILURE

M any years ago, during a strategy session with one of my clients while on a boating outing on Lake Austin, we decided he should bring on a COO to manage the daily operations of his growing company.

It was the right decision at the right time for the growth of his company. We interviewed half a dozen candidates; one stood out above the other prospects. It was the first time I took notes on the wisdom a candidate shared. My client and I were blown away and offered him the position which he accepted.

The CEO gave him a forty-thousand-foot overview of the Company, introduced him to the team, gave him the authority to make all day-to-day decisions, and granted him the keys to the kingdom.

On my next call with the CEO, he said his goal for the next few weeks was to stay out of the way and let the new COO take charge. I was not comfortable with his decision, but he insisted it was the best way to empower the new COO. The truth was the CEO was burnt out, looking for a savior, and wanted to run away from the everyday demands of his business.

What happened next was a total disaster.

Over the next three months, the new COO:

- Proved to be a terrible listener
- Showed favoritism
- Sabotaged the morale of a great culture
- Was responsible for several great talents quitting
- Alienated several key clients

As a result, the company lost money for the first time in over three years.

On my next visit, I met with the new COO. It was evident he was way in over his head. I was stunned to learn how little he understood the business and its financial model. It was an IT software company that implemented Microsoft software solutions for their clients.

They also sold products as part of their model, but there was little margin in them. The COO bragged that he decided to lower the prices of their services because the real money was in selling products.

I interviewed key members of the team who felt as though the CEO had abandoned them and handed the company over to an arrogant person with poor leadership skills and no integrity or concern for the team. I relayed this to the CEO. We arranged a meeting with the COO and fired him on the spot.

It could all have been avoided if the CEO:

- Had taken the time to train the new COO
- Had made a job scorecard for the COO
- Had established KPIs for the COO
- Had daily huddles and weekly meetings with him
- Stayed in the loop on the crucial decisions
- Talked with his team to ask how the transition was going
- Set performance goals
- Observed the COO's behaviors - the leading indicator of results

- Had not gone radio silent

There were many lessons here.

Lesson #1: Everyone coming into a leadership position needs to be trained, coached, or mentored and not set up for failure. It's front-end loaded.

Lesson #2: The CEO or manager must take responsibility to ensure they have the right person in the job and this person is given every opportunity to succeed. Within ninety days or less, you should know if you've made the right choice. If the answer to the question "Knowing what I know now, would I hire the person again?" is no, then let them go!!!

Final thought, please beware that if you are burned out or fatigued, you are likely to make poor decisions.

THREE ESSENTIALS TO
SUCCESSFUL NEGOTIATIONS

A major initiative one of my clients had was to solidify an all-star, can-do team. The good news was people trusted him. They saw the extraordinary results of his work. They loved working with him and wanted to be part of a rocket ship where the sky was the limit.

We had finalized negotiations with all core team members and all but one key strategic partner. The other one is more complicated, is a work in progress, and we are all committed to making it work.

In each round of negotiation, we shared our appreciation of their talent, results, and experience. We also discussed our vision of their role in the company's growth.

They shared what they needed to commit to us as full-time team members or as a designated strategic partner.

One person, who worked full-time for another company, and part-time for us, suggested a figure to us to substantiate leaving the full-time position. This figure was out of our reach of what we could justify for the position. When we asked him to explain how he derived the number, he said he needed to cover health insurance and taxes. We explained that the company now offered health benefits. In addition, the company would pick up the employer's portion of his taxes. That reduced his number by about 25%. When all was said and done, we shared how we could match the remainder of his number with performance-based bonuses on future projects, and he could have about forty hours a week of his life back.

Another player we wanted was a top-notch designer. He wanted a set fee for his design projects and a 10% royalty. YIKES! In our conversation, he said that working with us would be the equivalent of him being Walt Disney, the creator, and us being brother Roy Disney, the guy that was the strategic, business, and financial genius. It was clear that he wanted the alliance with us to solidify his future.

We asked for clarification if the 10% royalty was based on gross or net sales. He said 10% of the net. That was something we could do, and we had a deal.

In both cases, what appeared to be a bridge too far to gap and what almost caused us not to bother to negotiate was a lack of clarity on what the other side wanted. It would have been easy to walk, but instead, we decided to talk and ask questions.

We came to realize that unsophisticated negotiators do not know how to clarify what they want and need

We were thrilled we found the win-win and could add both of their considerable talents to our team at a compensation structure we could afford.

The key ingredients to successful negotiations are: Talking, listening, and asking questions. Why? So that we can understand what the other party wants and needs in return for their time and skills.

DELEGATE TO ELEVATE

⚜

"If something can be done 80% as well by someone else, delegate!" - John C. Maxwell

"I 'd rather do it myself."

"No one can do it better."

"I don't want to waste my time teaching someone else to do it when it's just so much easier for me to do it, and it's done, done, and done."

Throughout my career, I've heard these sentiments thousands of times.

Spoiler alert: IT IS NOT A SCALABLE MINDSET! It is a recipe for carrying all the monkeys on your back and it is not sustainable.

Healthy sustainable growth doesn't happen without the best people in the right seat. No one can do it all, **NO ONE!** (Pun intended) You are in the hiring, requiring, inspiring, training, and communications business.

Great leaders teach, inspire, hold people accountable, lead by example and earn the right to hold others to a higher standard.

The best people request the following things of their leaders:

- To give them more skills
- To make them more valuable
- To trust them to grow and learn from their mistakes
- To challenge and mentor them
- To hold them accountable

As the old proverb goes, *"If you give a man a fish, you feed him for a day. If you teach a man to fish, you feed him for a lifetime."*

If you teach me how to fish, I can grow my skills and become more valuable.

If you teach me how to fish, I can bring you fish for dinner.

If you teach me how to cook, I can make the fish for dinner.

If you teach me how to cook, I can prepare dozens of other meals.

Teaching someone valuable skills will be nourishing for everyone involved.

I once had a client who issued the invoices and did the payroll and accounts receivable for his multi-million-dollar company. I inquired why he didn't let someone else do it.

His response was "I can do it as well as anyone else." I gently challenged, "Then why don't you take on all the job responsibilities you do as well as everyone else's?" That got his attention.

I asked:

1. How many hours per week do you work?
2. How much of your time and energy do you focus on the activities that will enhance market share, build a great team, and enhance the top and bottom line?
3. What is it costing you in lost opportunities by not focusing on growing your business?
4. How much of your time do you spend on trivial tasks?

5. How much time do you devote to your family?
6. Are you having fun?
7. What is the highest and best use of your talent?
8. Are you confusing the illusion of being busy with the importance of putting your time and energy where you and the company will receive the most significant return?

We have only so much bandwidth. Where do you want to put your time and energy? How many unnecessary extra hours are you adding to your working day and taking away from your life?

One of the first tests of leadership is to be able to delegate.

- Delegate to accelerate productivity
- Delegate to elevate the skills of your team
- Delegate to celebrate the creative collaboration of working with others

If it's a job you hate, delegate.

"The first rule of management is delegation. Don't try and do everything yourself because you can't." - Anthea Turner

THE SECOND PART OF
DELEGATING

Anyone who manages people needs to master the skill of delegating. The second phase of delegating is to hold others accountable, and **it's essential.**

Successful communication is in the throw. Take the time to make sure your request is clear. Make sure what you want is understood. Failing to establish clarity is the number one source of miscommunication. **It's the communicator's responsibility to convey the message.** I can't catch the ball if you don't throw it to where I can catch it.

Remember that paraphrasing leads to clarity. Ask the person you're delegating to paraphrase what you requested or write it in an email to you. That is how you know if your message is clear and what you want is understood.

Establishing timelines and prioritizing will ensure deadlines are met. Create a timeline for achieving the task and get buy-in on whether your deadline is achievable. What priority are you establishing for the project? Measure the importance of any project against existing initiatives.

Require that you are kept in the loop. Schedule time for updates on the project's process in advance. **The burden should be on the other person to keep you in the loop** on what is completed and what is a work in progress. You don't want to be wasting your time chasing them for updates.

If there are bottlenecks, you want to know immediately. You don't want to be blindsided later and learn a deadline isn't met or the project has been scrapped.

Recognize and praise results. The most effective way to reinforce positive behaviors is to praise them.

If you pass the baton of responsibility to someone and give them a new role or responsibility, establish specific times to review and provide feedback on their efforts.

Don't set anyone up for failure. If it's the right person, the time you spend upfront training and coaching them will save you hundreds of hours overtime.

ONE DOOR OPENS ANOTHER

Think of your network as your community. We get together and get ahead by establishing a connection with people in our lives who will be there for us, just as we are for them. The best networkers understand the wisdom of taking the long view. They genuinely enjoy establishing relationships and friendships with peers and people they admire. They are givers, and as a result, people give to them in return.

The benefits of networking lead to:

- **Referrals** - Introductions to people that you can help or who can help you. Connecting people is one of my greatest joys. Eighty percent of my current clients came from referrals.
- **Sounding board** - People who can be a source for advice and feedback. You can count on them to give you perspective and to have your best interests at heart.
- **Information** - Learning from your network based on their acquired wisdom, experience, and expertise.
- **Support and encouragement** - People who are there for you when you need them the most.
- **Positive Energy** - We all need positive energy. What a gift to be able to lift someone when they are down.

Building a network is like gardening. We plant a seed and, like plants and flowers, relationships blossom if we take the initiative and put in the effort to keep them alive. The network you create is a garden worthy of cultivating.

WHAT'S YOUR BATNA?

M any years ago, I spoke with two entrepreneurs who were entering negotiations for promising opportunities.

I asked each to share with me their BATNA. Both looked perplexed and asked, "What's a BATNA?"

Roger Fisher and Scott Brown coined the term in their classic book on negotiation *Getting to Yes: Negotiating Agreement Without Giving In.* BATNA stands for the "Best Alternative to a Negotiated Agreement."

In negotiation theory, the best alternative to a negotiated agreement or BATNA refers to the most advantageous alternative course of action you can take if negotiations fail, and an acceptable agreement cannot be reached. It is sometimes referred to as the "no-deal option."

Attractive alternatives are needed to develop a strong BATNA, and the authors give three suggestions on how to accomplish this:

1. Create a list of actions you might take if an agreement is not advantageous.
2. Convert some of the more promising ideas and transform them into tangible and partial alternatives.
3. Determine the next best option.

95

An entrepreneur from El Salvador was considering a strategic relationship with a company from another country. They were both working in the billboard industry and were discussing whether they wanted to combine forces to create digital billboards together.

In light of new information, the entrepreneur had doubts about the purpose of a meeting in Guatemala. I suggested he take the weekend to think about it. That Monday, he said he had changed his mind and wanted to cancel the meeting. I asked if he thought there might be other opportunities for them to work together. The two met and came away from their meeting with ideas for different ways that they could work together. It was important for this client to spend some time considering what he actually wanted out of the relationship and being clear on this when they met.

Another scenario was of an entrepreneur of a baby products business who was in negotiation with a major distributor of her product. They gave her a ten-page contract in small print. One of the clauses was they would receive ninety-day terms plus a two percent discount.

There is no direct competition for her product, and there are other buyers in the space willing to meet her terms.

If she accepts those terms, it can put her out of business. So, her BATNA may well be to walk away or:

- Consider a line-of-credit from a bank tied to receivables to give her cash immediately for their orders.
- Then, demand a guaranteed order size.
- She can insist that as they are a small company, their standard contract is net thirty, and they only give discounts for cash upon delivery.
- She can sell to the major distributor's competition to generate the same revenue.

This enabled her to set boundaries. Just knowing that she could walk if she did not receive acceptable terms gave her confidence and put her in the driver's seat.

My guess is by holding firm to her BATNA, she will either negotiate a deal she can accept or walk from a deal that would otherwise jeopardize her business. Either one is a positive outcome.

Knowing your BATNA ensures that you have gone through a critical thinking process and will make the best decision for you.

TRENDSETTERS & FOLLOWERS

❦

Recently Moe and I had the pleasure of facilitating a retreat for Lekker Home, the #1 source for warm modern furniture in the USA. Their signature collection is eye candy for anyone who appreciates designs that are as beautiful as they are functional. Co-owner and founder Natalie Carpenter is the major procurator of the collection. She continually searches for everything from sofas, chairs, and tabletop settings to handmade glass from the Czech Republic and two-foot-tall colorful, one-of-a-kind, weaved baskets from Africa.

It's not uncommon for buyers from retail competitors to shop their showroom and website for ideas and products to seek out and sell.

When I owned R&R Junction, other retailers shopped at our store for products to source, and within a year, we'd see these products on the shelves of our competition. One of my vendors once said, "If it makes you feel better, imitation is the highest form of flattery, and they will also copy your mistakes as well because they won't know the difference."

R&R's customers came primarily from Washington D.C., Pittsburg, Richmond, and towns and cities within a 200-mile radius of Nags Head, N.C., and that made it easy to be trendsetters to our clients.

We discovered that most trends for the merchandise we sold originated in Europe, and from there, they went to the west coast, then NYC and Chicago before they hit the rest of the U.S.

We strategically attended trade shows in San Francisco and bought "hot new merchandise." As a result, we were able to spot trends as far as two years out and still be the first to introduce them to the east coast. For example, we introduced pink coral jewelry, mined in the deep waters off Hawaii, two years before you could find the collection in Bloomingdale's and Neiman Marcus.

Some products or services are around for years before they reach the tipping point. For example, when Moe and I were in Bali, Indonesia, and Melbourne, Australia, Moe noticed fashionable women wearing false eyelashes. Today, one of our clients is Cherry Lash, founded by Reyna Nebeker over a decade ago. There are two Cherry Lash salons in Las Vegas that have a local following and are a must-visit for many fashionable ladies in Las Vegas. They are now innovators riding the wave of a fashion trend whose time has arrived, and expansion plans are in the works.

If you look for trends, you'll find them everywhere. Within the next year, members of our Food for Thought community will buy an electric bike, be regulars at an eyelash salon or participate in an *Ayahuasca* ceremony. Oh, you already have? You trendsetter you!

THE 11 KEY COMPONENTS OF A FINANCIAL STRATEGY FOR GROWING A COMPANY

Most budding entrepreneurs focus on creating a strategic growth plan. Few create a financial strategy to go hand in hand with their business strategy. This often leads to companies finding themselves running out of capital because they did not create a financial strategy based upon conservative projections.

It is devastating when a company runs out of cash or finds itself in debt which eats away at revenue and drains cash flow. Sooner or later debt must be paid back.

Below are 11 critical questions to guide you in developing your financial strategy and creating realistic cash flow projections. Putting the time and focus into answering these questions can be the difference between growing smart or failing miserably.

1. What is your long-term vision?
2. Where do you want to take your business?
3. What resources will you need to accomplish these goals?
4. What is the real cost of growth?
5. What is the cost of acquiring capital (time and dollars)?
6. What is the cost of capital, including debt service and giving up equity?

7. What is the cost of changing or expanding your business focus? What are the risks (and lost opportunities) of not growing?
8. How do you guarantee the cash flow necessary to meet the daily, weekly, and monthly obligations of your company?
9. Do you have state-of-the-art systems in place to maximize purchasing dollars and collections?
10. Do you have the appropriate incentive programs in place to attract and retain quality personnel, including bonuses, benefits, and retirement plans?
11. Do you have the right risk management programs in place to protect your company against catastrophes and interruption of normal business?

No matter where you are in the growth of your business, it's never too early to answer these questions.

Savvy entrepreneurs consider it a necessity to answer questions like these. They take time to create a financial strategy before moving forward with the strategic plan. If you need help to create it, reach out to experts who can walk you through the process.

When you control your money, you control your future.

THE ART OF WRITING EMAILS

Before you hit send!

One and out usually doesn't cut it when writing an email. Emails are often misunderstood and poorly written. They can be unclear and lack courtesy and professionalism. Over the last couple of years, I have added communication, via email, to my communication workshops.

Below are examples of two emails I tweaked for the general manager of a company.

Subject: Manufacturing Meeting Reminder

FYI Manufacturing Meeting Thursday 3/22/21. Please be on time and prepared. **I want** to have a brief typed summary of what you discussed to keep in my record. **I want** this summary handed in at the end of the meeting. Thanks.

Subject: Manufacturing Meeting 3/22/21

Looking forward to seeing everyone at the Manufacturing Meeting on Thursday, March 22. To respect everyone's time, please mark it on your calendars and make sure to be there when we start.

It will be extremely helpful if you have a brief typed summary regarding what you will be presenting. Please be prepared to hand this in at the end of each meeting. These meetings are the cornerstone in achieving alignment on our goals and initiatives.

Thank you.

Subject: Quarterly Manufacturing Meeting

<u>I</u> reached out to the sales team to get feedback on the manufacturing needs for the coming year.

I'm requesting that all departments (Engraving, Tool Room, Engineering) be prepared to present at the upcoming meeting.

I am also soliciting information from the production staff to make sure we are addressing any issues they may have moving forward.

I'm striving to have a more aligned and engaged effort this upcoming year. I would appreciate any feedback you may have on my approach!

Subject: Quarterly Manufacturing Meeting

Last week the sales team gave great feedback on how the manufacturing group can enhance communications and performance with them for the upcoming year. Can't wait to share with you.

All departments (Engraving, Tool Room, Engineering) are preparing to present at the upcoming meeting.

The production staff is gathering information about any issues they face to proactively address these moving forward.

This way we are more aligned and engaged as a team in the upcoming year. Any thoughts or feedback you may have will be greatly appreciated!

Key point: *It's "We," not "Me" or "I."* Make the team feel involved and valued by showing that you are considering their priorities and time in the email too, not just your own.

I encourage you to try this four-step approach and see if it makes a difference.

1. **First Draft:** Get your thoughts out, write it all down.
2. **Review:** Edit, make changes to give the email character, and be sure it conveys what you want to communicate.
3. **Re-read:** Go over with fresh eyes.
4. **Finalize and before you hit SEND, review one last time:** If it's a criticism or you are writing an angry message, sit on it until the next day and ask yourself is email the best way to communicate this message. If not, pick up the phone and actually speak to another human being.

WHAT WOULD YOU PAY TO HAVE YOUR LIFE BACK?

I always look forward to having calls with a client from whom I can learn. Below, for example, is a conversation one of my clients, a CEO, had with one of his key team members.

For context, this particular team member never embraced the concept of delegating. He believed he needed to take care of all his department's responsibilities. In fact, a few weeks prior, he interrupted his vacation several times to take calls from potential and current clients.

The CEO saw this as an opportunity to ask him, "How much would you pay to have your life back? How much would you pay to **NOT** be at the beck and call of every request?" He got the message.

There are many ways for us to "give away our lives" by getting stuck in the thick of thin stuff and the belief that "*only I can do it.*"

In my view, this belief is a myth that significantly costs us both creative and free time. There are several reasons we talk ourselves into this trap.

No one can do it better than me.

Even if this is true, so what?! You only have so much bandwidth. You can do anything you want, but you can't do everything you want.

It's easier to do it myself.

Training and passing off a task or responsibility is front-end loaded. It may cost you time initially, but once you teach someone, you can focus on more high-hanging fruit.

There's no cost if I do it.

Wanna bet? How about the cost of lost opportunities? If your time is worth several hundred dollars an hour, why waste it doing a job that pays under $25 per hour? Do the math. Would you like to have more time to spend with your family and friends? Would you like to travel or read a book or take a cooking course? Every minute you spend doing one thing is a minute spent not doing something else.

Who has the time to train someone to take the burden off my plate?

YOU do because **you are NOT scalable.** Nor is it sustainable. Sooner or later, you will burn out.

If it's a job you hate, delegate.

Put your time and energy in your Zone of Genius. The activities that give you energy and have the greatest return, not the ones that take up your time while zapping your energy.

Embrace the 87% rule.

If a team member does the job the way you would 87% of the time, as long as the other 13% does not violate the company's values, **let it go.**

As Steven Stills wrote, "Find the cost of freedom." Teach your team well and write the check.

SIX BLIND MEN AND AN
ELEPHANT

""If I insist on giving you my truth and never stop to receive your truth in return, there can be no truth between us." - Thomas Merton

The parable of the *Six Blind Men and an Elephant* originated in the ancient Indian subcontinent. It is a story of a group of blind men who live in a small village in India. One day someone brings a gentle elephant to the village and invites everyone to see and touch it, including the six blind men.

Each blind man touches a different part of the elephant's body, but only one part each. They then describe the elephant based on their limited experience. Their descriptions of the elephant are different from each other. In some versions, they come to suspect that the other person is dishonest, and they come to blows. The moral of the story is that humans tend to claim absolute truth based on their limited, subjective experience and ignore other people's limited, personal experiences, which may be equally valid.

As a startup grows, it will eventually reach what we called at INC. Magazine, the "second stage of growth." While the first stage is mainly sales and mission-driven, this second stage is the operational phase where systems and processes are created, and departments begin to emerge. It's an exciting time for most businesses. The mantra that 'everyone does everything' gives way to specialization.

Stage three is the transition stage where the best lead companies transition from a mom-and-pop business to a professional company. However, in this stage, communication systems tend to break down, and departments don't communicate well, which can result in finger-pointing, poor morale, and low productivity.

The challenge, for department leaders, is not to become like the six blind men.

"Great performance is 1% vision and 99% alignment." - Jim Collins

ONE WAY OF LOOKING AT RELATIONSHIPS

 ∞

BY GUEST CONTRIBUTOR RACHEL WEISBERG

R ecently I had a coaching call with one of Rich's client's assistants. The conversation meandered across many aspects of being a good assistant and support person to an executive. But one thing kept bubbling up in my mind: **This is a relationship**.

In fact, it's an intimate one. Yes, it's a working relationship, but it's so much more than that. It requires as much attention as a romantic relationship or a dear friendship. It requires listening, providing feedback, receiving feedback, and acting on it.

The benefits of treating any relationship as a true relationship are manyfold:

1. When you get to know someone well (i.e., in a relationship), trust grows.
2. When you trust someone, you naturally respect each other AND each other's time.
3. When there is mutual respect, you are careful with your words and actions.
4. When you are careful with words and actions, the message is (almost always) clear.

5. When the message is clear, there are fewer misunderstandings or missteps.
6. When there are fewer misunderstandings or missteps, people are happy!

Happy is the goal!

Of course, workplace relationships come in all kinds. Many of us form strong, lasting relationships with teammates that last beyond the workplace. I can count on one hand, the people I've worked with in the past who are still dear friends. One, in particular, I've had in my life for upwards of 20 years! I still include her in my list of references even though we haven't worked together since 2006.

Sometimes your teammates are just that, teammates. We don't have to love everyone we work with - if you're lucky enough to, then wahoo! However, WE DO HAVE TO RESPECT everyone we work alongside. When we treat each relationship like a relationship, it helps facilitate things with greater ease.

This extends beyond the workplace, too. When you treat the world as your friend, the benefits still apply.

So, I challenge you to the following:

- Put as much effort into your interactions with the cashier, at the grocery store, as you would your best friend.
- Use his or her name and ask how their day is going.
- Do your best to be present with your teammates.
- Take a moment to slow down with your child's daycare teacher, your pharmacist, or your UPS delivery person.
- Spend the time to get to know people around you and then watch your world unfold into a more connected, productive, fun, and happier place.

WHO ARE YOUR FUTURE LEADERS

Yesterday I facilitated a training session with a leadership team. The company has two locations. Over the next 18 months, they plan to open a franchise and another corporate store. Our focus in this training session was to establish other leaders in the company with the skills and the training to step up when required.

Following Jim Collins's model in his book, *Good to Great*, we began with a question. Were all team members "A" players? An "A" player is dependable, does their job well, and their actions support the company's values. The good news was that, across the board, there were "A" players at every position. We identified two employees who were not team players.

Next, we assessed who among the team had the potential to manage a department or a store. We identified at least six team members who had the right skills and attitudes.

We also considered establishing a company advisory board that would consist of team members from our list of potential leaders. This is a great way to access potential leadership talent in action for any company.

It was an exciting meeting. It proved invaluable to the company to assess the team and to identify its future leaders. The next step was to create a program to groom and train them.

I recommend that every company take the time to assess and identify your roster of talent and create a path for growth from within.

AND THE X FACTOR IS?

In January of 2020, Moe and I facilitated a retreat for the wonderful Stateside Agency, a nearshore technology company in Costa Rica. They build and maintain websites and mobile devices, and provide digital marketing and staff implementation for international Fortune 10,000 companies.

In business, an X-Factor is a variable that can have the most significant impact on a company's success. The leadership team of Stateside Agency determined that the company's X Factor, in a very competitive market, is staff retention.

Staff turnover is a hidden cost that does not appear on a profit-and-loss statement but is disruptive, expensive, and time-consuming. Replacing an employee requires additional recruiting, interviewing, testing, training, lost knowledge, ramp-up time, and there is always the potential that the new employee will not be the right fit. And if that's not enough, staff turnover impacts the morale of a team.

Studies consistently show that money is number seven on the list of why people work for a company.

What people want most is what's referred to as "psychic income."

The six basics of psychic income are:

1. *Recognition and Pride*

We all want our work to be recognized and appreciated. Great leaders and managers catch people doing something right and show their appreciation by letting them know it.

2. *Emotional Security*

People leave people, not companies. No one wants to be bullied, disrespected, or continuously criticized. Or be in a job with responsibilities that set us up for failure. Praise in public, criticize constructively in private.

3. *We want to be heard*

When we interview our clients' staff, we often find that the best ideas for growth and solutions to problems are already there in the hearts and minds of people who care but are not asked to share or are not listened to.

4. *We want to be in the loop*

The first sign of a negative culture is people having to depend on gossip or hearsay to know what's going on.

It's not that hard for leaders and managers to take the time to share information. At the very least, we want to know where we stand and expect annual reviews to occur consistently, with feedback in between. I'm a believer in quarterly evaluations. Annual reviews lose their purpose and importance when they are combined with raises and bonuses.

5. *Training and Development*

Companies that provide career paths and opportunities for individual growth through training and career development have the highest retention rates of "A players." Great talent wants to be continuously challenged, taught new skills, and given opportunities for advancement.

6. *Economic Security*

Employees want the company they are working for to be on a solid financial footing. They don't want to worry about the company closing down, being laid off, or whether they'll receive their next paycheck.

Companies that reward their associates with psychic income have the best chance of keeping them.

BEING OUR BEST

⁂

In the 1992 movie, Mr. Baseball, an aging professional baseball player, Jack Elliot (played by Tom Selleck), is traded to a Japanese league. Unhappy with his career, he rejects the local customs and clashes with his new teammates. But, in time, he learns to appreciate his new home.

In a defining moment in the movie, Tom Selleck says, "What I've learned from the Japanese culture is, when I try not to miss the ball, I swing and miss. When I try to meet the ball, I hit it."

You can't miss when you're in the zone, whether you're a speaker, writer, musician, craftsperson, artist, or athlete.

The best companies and individuals have something in common - a can-do attitude and culture. They believe in themselves, and they always give their best. Can-do means will do, every time. Their confidence is based upon their pride in their performance and exceeding expectations.

What does it take to perform at your best?

- A good night's sleep
- Proper preparation

- Being in your Zone of Genius
- Fuel - the right food in your body
- Adrenaline
- Enthusiasm
- Positive energy
- A dedicated support team
- A commitment to excellence

I invite you to ask yourself what it takes for you to be at your best. Stack the deck in your favor. Every day is showtime and your opportunity to shine.

COMPETITION? BRING IT ON!!!

꧂

My grocery store of choice in Chapel Hill, NC, is The Fresh Market. Within a five-minute drive, I can shop at Wegmans, Trader Joe's, and Harris Teeter. I can get yellow peppers at Food Lion for a buck less than The Fresh Market. The same applies to many of the staples I buy. Readers of USA Today voted The Fresh Market their #1 supermarket choice for 2021. Why is this if it doesn't offer the lowest prices? For me, it's the overall shopping experience, the quality of what they sell from meats to seafood, to fruits and wine, and the service is first class.

The grocery store brand is cheaper than the other brands, yet people buy Heinz's ketchup and French's mustard and all sorts of brand products that are more expensive.

There can be two gasoline stations, across the street from one another, one sells gas at $2.89 per gallon, and the other at $2.59 per gallon. Yet, why do people choose the gasoline brand that's 30 cents more? It is because it's easier to get to, or you have a credit card that gives you points from a brand, or if you're like me, you boycott Exxon or BP because of how they handled environmental spills.

A friend who owns a jewelry store always wants his store located next to a Macy's. Why? Because Macy's draws traffic, he is confident he could compete with them. It's the same reason why there are twenty restaurants on Restaurant Row or thousands of wholesalers and retailers in the Jewelry district in NYC.

Merchants sell their goods online on Amazon, the largest marketplace in the world, and adjust their prices or offerings to stay competitive. On Amazon, it goes with the territory. If you are afraid of competition, it's because you either do not have a competitive advantage or you're afraid people will steal your ideas. They will, so don't take it personally. The solution is to go for a short-term competitive advantage, create a loyal following, offer the lowest price or the highest value, build brand loyalty, establish great relationships, or make your money in the buying.

There are many ways to stay competitive. Competition can make you better, savvier and keep you from becoming complacent. The old mantra was, "Are you better, faster, or cheaper?" You used to get to pick one. The new mantra is "You must be all of the above."

The marketplace is not for the timid; it is always changing. You can approach it like an art form or science. Either way, those who thrive say, "Competition? Bring it on!!!"

THE EXECUTION TEMPLATE IN THE WILD

⊗

On May 13th, 2022, Moe and I will have as our guests, the McBride brothers and sisters together, Daniel Dunlavey, Timothy Patrick, Kevin Francis, Sean Kearny, and Sheila Ann, in our beautiful home in Chapel Hill, N.C. This would be the first time since the start of the pandemic.

As a result of our decision to strictly remain in voluntary quarantine (or shelter in place), until we were vaccinated, dozens of repair and beautification projects for our home were put on hold.

These included:

- Framing and hanging artwork
- Landscaping
- Repairing fixtures in bathrooms
- Fixing the on switch on our jacuzzi
- Adding solar lighting in our driveway
- Hanging tapestries
- Fixing the front door lock
- Hanging a Japanese tapestry on the wall beside the staircase
- Making sure we have enough bedding for everyone

- Buying an extra blow-up bed
- Purchasing throw pillows for our sofa
- Purchasing an 8' round oriental style rug for under the entranceway table
- Completing an exterminator spring outdoor service

All of these will be completed before the arrival of the McBride clan. That's the power of a mission and deadlines you are committed to achieving.

The book "Execution: The Discipline of Getting Things Done" by Larry Bossidy and Ram Charan gives you a step-by-step template on what it takes to master the art of execution.

STEP 1 - Define the Mission

Rich & Moe's Step 1 = Complete checklist before the Mc Bride clan's arrival.

STEP 2 - Create a drop-dead deadline

Wednesday, May 12th, a day before their arrival

STEP 3 - Assign/Identify who owns the project and who needs to be involved (internally and outside services)

Moe owns the project. I am second-in-command. In addition, we have engaged the following outside resources:

- Our handyman team, Juan and Alison
- The landscaper, Aubrey
- The cleaning crews
- Picture framing and matting store
- Groceries to feast upon for the McBride's
- Organizer specialist for closets and drawers
- Exterminator

STEP 4 - Determine why it is important

So that everything is in harmony and working when our guests arrive.

STEP 5 - Everyone is clear on drop-dead deadlines and is committed to meeting them.

Rich and Moe have agreed on the drop-dead date and have arranged for the above services to be completed prior to this date, allowing time for potential delays.

STEP 6 - What's the budget?

$4,500 - landscaping is expensive.

To prevent scope creep, i.e., the addition of extra services that will increase costs, we have clearly stated what we want to our service providers. We have pre-arranged the specific services they will provide and the fee we will pay.

We decided that we did not have enough time to shop for a sofa bed and that it was way out of our budget - so we reconsidered our plan and decided not to purchase a sofa bed.

STEP 7 - If milestones are missed, have a Plan B.

Juan and Alison were our plan B Handyman team. They are extremely diligent and reliable.

STEP 8 - How will we know the project is completed?

All our objectives are met.

STEP 9 - What will be the benefits?

The loose ends and beautification projects we wanted to do and enjoy for the last year are complete. I won't need a workaround to light up the grill. Our "love tub" will be working again.

STEP 10 - How will you celebrate?

Welcoming the McBride clan into our home for laughter, reminiscing, and creating new memories and perhaps an annual Chapel Hill visit as a new ritual.

Faithfully following the Execution Template gets it done every time.

LET'S PLAY IN THE SHARK TANK

Recently I was working on a project to help a client prepare a submission application for Shark Tank, a US reality TV show where aspiring entrepreneurs pitch their business ideas to a panel of potential investors. To appear on the show, you first have to submit a video application of your business idea. If the producers like your pitch, you are selected to come on the show.

My clients are a married couple who own a manufacturing business for baby swaddle blankets and accessories. During our first recorded rehearsal, I read them the questions, and they answered. Then we reviewed the recordings, made corrections, and decided what to tweak, what to add, and what to remove.

During the second rehearsal, the couple began playing off each other, this led to exchanges of smiles, more animated body language, and they were glowing with the love and respect they have for each other. Watching them play off each other was adorable and captivating. The third time was the charm. By showing their personalities, their love for and belief in the product shone through. They are waiting to hear back.

The Shark Tank submission video instructions outline all the important tips for creating your elevator pitch. And the advice isn't just applicable if you want to be on the show, **this is how you should talk about your product/business in every situation.** See below:

THE SHARK TANK GUIDE TO MAKING A SUBMISSION VIDEO

"Please make a short video (5 to 10 minutes) to talk about yourself and show off your personality. Wow us! Dazzle us! Be talkative and energetic! Don't be humble. It's your opportunity to gloat and convince us why you are perfect for the show. "

"I want to add that this video is your only chance to impress everybody, making it great. Below are tips on how to make the video:

All collaborators may appear together in a single audition video.

BE SURE TO ANSWER ALL OF THESE QUESTIONS IN YOUR VIDEO. If you are applying as a team, then everybody needs to appear on the video if they want to appear on the program."

1. What's your name, where are you from, and what do you do for a living?

2. What is your business/product? Start by saying, "My business is..." and then clearly describe what your business or product is exactly.

(THIS IS THE MOST IMPORTANT! WE NEED TO CLEARLY UNDERSTAND WHAT YOUR BUSINESS OR PRODUCT IS!)

3. How much money do you need from investors, and what percentage of your company/idea/product are you willing to give up (e.g., 10%, 40%, etc.)? Be specific. Simply say "I'm seeking $_____ in exchange for _____%." Note: You may later change your requested ask if you appear on the program

4. How will the money be used? BE SPECIFIC.

5. Please describe your product/business. (THIS IS VERY IMPORTANT)

a. What is so exciting or unique about your product/business? What is your HOOK? Your hook is key to a compelling pitch so explain this with lots of energy!!!

b. Why will people feel they must have your product/business?

c. Is it fully patented, or is the patent pending?

d. How far along is the development of your business/product? Is it just an idea, a working prototype/business plan, or is it an existing product or business currently on the market?

e. Is your product or business currently making money? If so, how much revenue has the product or company generated?

f. How or why does it work? (Do a demonstration if you can.)

g. How is your product or business different from similar ideas? What makes yours unique or better?

h. How did you come up with the idea? Explain your A-HA moment and share your story! You're the person behind the business, so celebrate yourself!

6. What are your sales? We need 2020 sales and 2021 projected year-end sales for 2021, and lifetime sales. Make sure you explain why your sales are what they are - whether they are high or low.

7. How much have you invested in your business/product?

8. What does your business/product mean to you?

9. Tell us something interesting about yourself.

10. What has been your biggest challenge so far?

PLEASE REMEMBER TO CLEARLY DESCRIBE WHAT YOUR PRODUCT OR BUSINESS IS, WHAT IT DOES, AND TO VISU-ALLY DEMONSTRATE YOUR PRODUCT/BUSINESS (if possible).

* SHOW YOUR PERSONALITY!

* Have "Infomercial" energy, and please stand up. Do not sit down while taping - it brings your energy down.

* Feel free to brag about any accolades you've received.

This is a great exercise for any company to do, and it could be a great contest for a forum or members of an association. There is a lot to cover in ten minutes, but it might be the best elevator pitch you ever create.

GROWING YOUR BUSINESS BEYOND 50 PEOPLE

BY GUEST CONTRIBUTOR RACHEL WEISBERG

G rowing a company has several challenges (and opportunities!) that have less to do with compliance and more to do with these 3 things:

1. Logistics
2. Communication
3. Cultural considerations

Below are some questions for a growing company:

- Do you have a plan for maintaining your culture?
- Where will people sit?
- Do you have the right people on the team? Are managers good at managing?
- What HR systems do you have in place?
- How will the team communicate?
- How do your benefits compare with other companies of the same size?

1. **Logistics - Space Planning:**

Granted, physical office spaces have changed dramatically since the pandemic began and have been evolving for a while. Once, the ideal was private offices. For a long time, companies maximized space with cubicles. From the mid-aughts onward, the preference has been the true open floor plan. Since the COVID pandemic in March 2020 forced businesses to close their offices for a few months, more and more employees have been working from home and coming into the office on a staggered basis, meaning less office space is required now than before.

It's important to think with a long-term vision when investing in office spaces. Space planners can help develop a plan with the flexibility to grow with your company.

Planning ahead is key! Quality office furniture often has a long turnaround time, so it's a good idea to get ahead of the need.

1. Communication - Hiring/Managers:

Some teams find that they have far too many people wearing too many hats, *especially* in HR. As a company grows, specialization and *clear responsibilities* are critical to each employee's success.

Take a good look at your organization's structure. Are your managers good at managing? It's never too early to train or retrain the people you want to be leaders and help them grow with the company - as Rich says, "Give people the opportunity to succeed, not fail!"

HR Systems:

What worked for 20 people won't always work for a larger team. Many companies have great success making it up as they go along, but once a team reaches the 50-person threshold, it's time to establish HR systems that work at scale.

The good news is there are Software as a Service (SaaS) products available, otherwise known as Human Resources Information Systems or HRIS. These products can help you manage payroll, reporting, and benefits. They can take all the grunt work out of onboarding and offboarding, help with recruitment, and streamline data management.

Communication Tools:

Communication may be less fluid within a larger team. Apps like Slack and WhatsApp allow for in-the-moment communication across teams. Video Conferencing programs like Zoom and Google Meet have transformed work during the global pandemic, allowing teams physically separated to work side-by-side.

3. Maintaining Company Culture:

"Culture" is a term bandied around a lot in the business world these days, but it's central to the identity of a company and the heart and soul of a team. It's the "special sauce" of a company, and if leadership is walking the talk, it trickles down and is something that employees can easily identify.

Benefits:

A big advantage of having a larger team is better prices on health benefits. Larger groups have better bargaining power, the carrier's risk is reduced, and companies can offer the employees more robust plans for less. Generous health benefits are non-negotiable these days and growing a team beyond 50 makes it easier.

As Rich mentioned in a previous post on *Phases of Growth*, making it to 50 employees often means a period of transformation/reinvention. Many systems that were in place before may not work, and the people who were the core of the company may not have the skills needed to manage their responsibilities (or may not want to. Some people prefer a small, scrappy, agile team and that's okay!).

This is a literal growing pain of growth. BUT with some planning and introspection about what makes your company tick, it can be a period of magic.

You can reach Rachel with any HR questions you have at Rachel@coachtothebest.com.

DON'T LET FEAR HOLD YOU BACK

I t's April, and it's a great time to do some mental spring cleaning. I invite you to start by throwing out the fears you have that hold you back from being all you desire to be. Let's say goodbye to the clutter taking up space in our minds and make room for confidence and courage.

The purpose of fear is to keep you safe. You want to get away from actual physical dangers, and fear compels us to take action. In these circumstances, fear is our friend. Fear of COVID led me to wear a mask, social distance, and not shop in person or travel over the past year.

Our inner fears come in all shapes and sizes. Thomas Oliver Kite Jr., an American professional golfer, writes that *"Fear comes in two packages. Sometimes the fear of failure and other times fear of success."*

Analytical personality styles struggle to make decisions or take action because their fear of failure haunts them and leads to analysis paralysis.

A Harvard study of the Board of Directors of Fortune 1000 companies concluded they prefer decisive leaders that make mistakes to leaders who are afraid or slow to make critical decisions. Great leaders are decisive but not impulsive.

The aim of Gay Hendrick's book *The Big Leap* is to teach how to "Conquer Your Hidden Fear and Take Life to the Next Level."

Understanding how the hidden fears of successful people lead to self-sabotage, including my own, was an epiphany for me. Hendricks identifies these fears as upper limit barriers. These perceived barriers are shaped early in our lives by the messages we receive from our parents, teachers, friends, schoolmates, and other family members.

Hendrick identifies four upper limit barriers:

- I'm not worthy
- The fear of outshining others
- Leaving others behind
- Being a burden on others

Gay and his wife, Kathlyn Hendricks, write that fear is harder to identify when it comes to relationships but is just as valid as the fear of physical danger.

In a recent article, Gay and Kathlyn identified two relationship-based fears. *"We've found that relationship-based fears (some call it "fear of intimacy") tend to come in two flavors. And both serve the same purpose: to keep you safe. Unfortunately, they also keep you from having a close, loving relationship."*

Relationship-Based Fear #1: Fear of Being Abandoned

"This one is familiar to most people. Being in a committed, loving relationship involves taking risks. To fully know another and create intimacy, you need to be vulnerable. The minute you commit to being with someone and being loved, you also open up the possibility of being left. It's a very scary premise. If you don't get too close, there's nothing to fear (or so we tell ourselves)."

Relationship-Based Fear #2: Fear of Being Smothered

"As much as you may genuinely want a lasting, loving relationship, part of you might be afraid that a relationship will take away your freedom."

"Being single comes with a lot of freedom - you get to decide what to do with your time and what your priorities are. The prospective of a close relationship presents another kind of threat: the potential loss of individuality, autonomy, and personal space."

Two of my favorite quotes are:

"Don't believe everything you think." - Alan Locus

"Fear stands for *False Evidence Appearing Real"* - Nick Vujicic

But I believe William Shakespeare said it best, "Our doubts are traitors, and make us lose the good we oft might win, by fearing to attempt."

Life is too precious to let hidden or false fears, in whatever form, keep us from living our lives to our fullest. Don't be afraid to fail, be afraid not to try. It's spring; spring forward fearlessly with love, courage, and self-confidence.

THE 7-7-7 CHALLENGE

Four Hands is a home furnishings design and wholesale company that grew by leaps and bounds. It had an incredible team of talented, conscientious, and "can do" personnel in virtually every position. The founder, Brett Hatton, had the courage and the conviction to embrace Jack Stack's philosophy of "open-book management" from the book *The Great Game of Business*.

The concept of open-book management is to engage employees in the inner workings of the business and keep them informed on the financial information of the company. Knowledge is power, and by sharing intricate details of the financial side of the company, employees feel trusted and empowered to take on more responsibility and contribute to the decision-making process.

Four Hands hired a specialist to teach their team how to read a financial statement and how to understand a profit and loss statement. The company did not share all of its financial information with its team, but more than enough to understand what it takes for the company to be profitable. Following Stack's model, Four Hands created a bonus program where everyone received bonuses based on its profitability.

As a result of the company's spectacular growth, everyone took their bonuses for granted until a devastating 4th Quarter wiped out all the profits of the first three quarters. This was because a significant client rejected an entire container of furniture due to poor quality issues. The company's quality assurance team did not do their job, and everyone took a financial hit. Everyone learned that profits are never guaranteed.

By the end of Q1 of the following year, Four Hands was rebounding. We decided to create a theme for Q2 focusing on achieving $7,000,000 in open orders, $7,000,000 in sales, and bringing $700,000 to the bottom line.

It was ambitious. The company had never brought 10% profits to the bottom line and had never had a $7,000,000 quarter. Matt Briggs, Four Hands current CEO, came up with the idea of calling it 7-7-7.

We created a T-shirt that we gave to all the employees with 7-7-7 designed to look like it was on a slot machine. We brought the entire company together to achieve buy-in and share what was in it for them if we reached our goals and why we thought it was possible. This made it feel like a 'great game of business', but with a real tangible prize at the end if the targets were met.

We started by asking the employees why they should care if the company was profitable. The consensus was:

- As the company grew, they would grow with it.
- Growth will create more opportunities for advancement in their career.
- There was a powerful sense of pride in being a part of Four Hands as it was emerging as a cutting-edge player in the furniture industry.
- It gave them financial security.
- A profitable Four Hands meant more profit sharing and more learning opportunities.

We educated everyone on where we were spending our money and how much we spent on salaries, benefits, training, and growth. The employees were surprised and gratified to see how much capital the company committed to their development, future, and income.

We asked everyone to brainstorm with their department members and answer three questions.

1. What can I do to reduce costs and/or help create more sales?
2. What can my department do?
3. What can the company do?

Each department picked a spokesperson to share:

1. What their action items were.
2. Who owned action items?
3. What were the timelines?
4. How would we measure success?

It was inspiring to see an entire company focused on answering these questions and how many solid ideas came out of it.

The 7-7-7 quarterly rock was a game-changer that resulted in its first double-digit bottom-line profits and highest revenue ever. And we created a Culture of Profitability.

Four Hands achieved this by creating buy-in, educating the team on where the company invested its money, challenging, measuring, and monitoring activity daily, and, lastly, establishing rewards to celebrate their success.

Everyone in the company received an increase in their bonus from $77 to $777. The company threw a kick-butt "Four Hands" style party with a rocking Austin live band, great food, wine, and beer. Everyone also received a card to pay for a cab, to and from the party, so no one had to worry about drinking and driving.

"You've got to change incentives for good behavior as opposed to just disincentivizing bad behavior." - Gavin Newsom

THE BENEFITS OF FINANCIAL
TRANSPARENCY

L ast week I was privileged to participate in two virtual leadership meetings where the CEO believed in their team enough to be transparent about the financial information of their company.

Later this month, Moe and I will be facilitating a retreat where the company CPA is part of the agenda. His role is to teach the team how to read a P&L and understand how their decisions affect its profitability.

In my experience, entrepreneurs that are comfortable sharing financial data benefit from leaders who feel trusted and have insight into the fundamental operations of the business. I am not advocating that entrepreneurs share individual salaries or the legitimate discretionary benefits entrepreneurs enjoy as a trade-off for taking all the risks and signing personally for business loans. Some numbers are private or personal.

In my program on *Creating a Culture of Profitability*, I begin by asking, "Why should you care about profitability?" The responses generate a framework for recognizing that profitability is essential to remain healthy and sustain growth.

Financial transparency leads to better decisions and a recognition of the importance of:

- Spending wisely.
- Minimizing waste and redundancy.
- Understanding and managing margins.
- Meeting and exceeding break-even numbers.
- The knowledge that increased salaries and bonuses can only come from profitability.
- Understanding that the cost of high growth is expensive.
- Acknowledging the total cost of salaries when you include health care, training, and other benefits.
- Recognizing that mistakes are costly.
- Knowing the difference between fixed and variable costs.
- Understanding that high variable costs like freight and oil in today's economy can diminish profitability.

Give your team members the challenge of finding ways to increase revenue, reduce costs and celebrate their success. You can create a thriving culture of profitability.

A FRENEMY IN NEED IS A FRIEND INDEED

America's new Secretary of State, Anthony Blinken recently said that "Our relationship with China will be competitive when it should be, collaborative when it can be, and adversarial when it must be."

It's a good mantra for entrepreneurs as well. There are many ways we can profitably collaborate with our competition.

In an agreement of game-changing magnitude, Merck, the American multinational pharmaceutical company, agreed to mobilize some of its factories to produce Johnson & Johnson's one-shot vaccine. As a result, there should be an adequate supply of the COVID vaccine for every adult American to get vaccinated by the end of May 2021. Imagine!

I worked with many clients who make a sizable portion of their revenue "selling to frenemies."

iTech Solutions in Houston provides their frenemies with technical skills for their commercial audio-visual projects.

Cincinnati Crane and Hoist manufactures overhead cranes and has the rare ability to manufacture and transport cranes up to seventy feet in length. They are the go-to solution for other crane manufacturers when they need cranes over sixty feet.

Thousands of companies white label their products or services. A white-label product is a product or service produced by one company that other companies rebrand to make it appear as if they had made it.

White label products populate the shelves of supermarkets, including Costco, Target, and Walmart, which compete side-by-side with their brand-name products. Think Kirkland products at Costco.

A company with competitive manufacturing advantages but no ability to promote and distribute its products may specifically design products branded by third parties.

Software services are frequently rebranded. It is common for business, infrastructure, and consumer information technology to be branded by multiple marketers. For example, a brand selling cloud computing services may be a reseller with no infrastructure or technical capabilities of its own.

The Richard Fischer Company makes elegant throw pillows by hand with the finest materials possible. The pillows sell for $300 each in the finest luxury stores in the world. Pier 1 Imports approached them to white label pillows that they then sold for more than double any other pillow they carried in their line.

Richard Fischer sold them the previous year's designs manufactured in China with lesser quality materials. They became Pier 1's most successful selling pillows and doubled Richard Fischer's revenue.

Selling to frenemies and white labeling your goods and services can make all the difference in your company's success. To shamelessly plagiarize Carole King, *"Winter, spring, summer, or fall, all you have to do is call and I'll be there - you've got a frenemy."*

WHAT DO CATCHING MY FIRST FISH AND PANDEMIC FATIGUE HAVE IN COMMON?

BY GUEST CONTRIBUTOR MAUREEN MCBRIDE

I was deeply in love---as deeply in love as any ten-year-old girl can be. How could I not be in love with the tall, blonde-haired, blue-eyed lead singer of the local singing group? The Delltones were a quartet of four handsome brothers who harmonized beautifully together.

David was an older man. He was twelve. We had thrown caution to the wind, and while we were walking in the woods one day, he reached down and - omg, omg, omg - held my hand! Can love be truer than when you are ten years old, and a boy holds your hand? *Sigh*

As our courtship progressed, he told me he wanted to take me fishing. (Or perhaps he wanted to go fishing, and I finagled my way into tagging along?)

I do remember being too squeamish to attach the earthworm to the hook. "Eww!"

The first fish I caught was also the last fish I caught.

There I stood giggling as my line started to jiggle with David instructing me how to bring the fish in. David told me we had no choice but to whack the fish against the water to knock it out so that we could remove the hook and set it free. The struggle felt quite intense at the time; however, this fish was too pitifully small to fry.

David showed me how to arc the pole, pull back, and cast, with the fish still on the hook. In theory, the fish would be knocked unconscious and feel no pain as we removed the hook and set the creature free. In his lesson, he had not emphasized the word "gently."

I wound up the thrust of my arm with the force of Sandy Koufax pitching a fastball, slamming the teeny tiny little fish against the water.

To my shock and horror, the guts of the fish spilled out and went drifting down the river. Later I shared with my father a dramatic rendition of the events of my first fishing episode. He laughed and said, "Eviscerated." (And then, of course, made me get the dictionary and look the word up with him).

Taking poetic license with the word 'evisceration', we can perhaps extend it to the sheer exhaustion and hollowing out of our center as we now go into our third year and fifth wave of pandemic infections. We hope with each wave that, THIS time, the information will be more accurate, while in reality, science is trying to jog on quicksand while the 24/7 news channels churn out partial news and new developments.

We are all a little hollowed out. We will regain our equilibrium, and a new normal will replace the old. Yes, this, too, will pass.

I hope you will share your patience and compassion with the people around you. All creatures great and small deserve a better fate than the first (and last) fish I ever caught. Slow down. Be kind. We are all a little bit eviscerated.

IN SEARCH OF KPIS

I was asked to speak to the sales team at Ortega Counseling in Los Angeles about the importance of Key Performance Indicators (KPIs). The company counsels employees who were disabled on the job. They place them in schools to get retrained for a new occupation. This program is funded by the State of California. Counselors match disabled workers with the right schools and the company pays for their training.

At the start of the session, I asked each team member to share what they would like to learn. One participant said that he'd never heard of KPIs in any other company he worked for and thought it was micro-management.

I saw he wore a facemask with a LA Dodgers logo on it. I asked him if he was a Dodgers fan, and he said yes.

"Who's your favorite pitcher on the Dodgers?" I asked.

"Clayton Kershaw," he replied.

"How many strikeouts does he average per game?" I asked.

"Ten."

"How many walks per game?" I continued.

"Four."

"How many pitches does he throw in a game?"

"One hundred."

"What's his lifetime Earned Run Average per game?"

"About 2.45, the best in Dodgers history."

"So how come you know Clayton Kershaw's KPIs, but you don't know your own?" I politely asked.

His answer was a good one.

"Because I don't know what my KPIs should be," he replied.

We all agreed that their ability to place their clients into schools is transformational to their clients, and they were committed to making it happen.

We determined that the most critical KPIs were the number of placements per month and that the minimum is 40 placements with a stretch goal of 60 placements. So, the KPI is 2-3 placements per day and 10-15 for the week. To achieve this, we needed to be working with about 25 qualified leads. So, the number of qualified leads is an obvious KPI.

We then got more specific. We agreed that there are three schools they generally recommend.

- One school is easy to work with and is always responsive. The KPI for contacts with that school was five.
- One is not quite as responsive, and the KPI or number of contacts for this school was ten.
- Finally, there was a school that was a fallback alternative and generally required at least fifteen contacts.

The good news was by staying the course; they were all viable choices.

We also broke the clients into 3 categories: a Karen, a Dolly, and a Casper.

Karen - Had lots of questions, was indecisive, and had to be followed up at least 15 times before finding a career option and school that was the right match.

Dolly - Easy as pie to place. Dolly clients always follow through and work with you to find the right match. With a Dolly client, after a few contacts, it's done, done, and done.

Casper - Like the friendly ghost, they disappear. You must constantly call them back to keep them focused and find the right match. It generally takes as many as 20 contacts to place a Casper and several agonizing months.

By the end of the call, we had KPIs for each salesperson, including the number of contacts to match each school and client. Defining and measuring these meaningful KPIs provides structure and purpose. They enable us to recognize when we are meeting or exceeding expectations, and they help us identify potential barriers when we aren't.

Key Performance Indicators

KPIs take all that inspirational language and help quantify it. You create them by asking a simple question "How would we know if we met our objective?"

Metrics can focus on:

- Growth
- Engagements
- Revenue
- Performance
- Quality

That last one can throw people. It doesn't seem very easy to measure quality. But quality can be measured by:

- Satisfaction ratings by our clients
- The number of clients that renew contracts
- Meeting our standards

With KPIs, you can balance forces like growth and performance or revenue and quality. With KPIs, you can be the Clayton Kershaw of your world.

FACE THE DANGER, COMMUNICATE WITH THE VENDOR

❦

"They pay as slow as cat piss and are as good as gold." - Judith Rosenberg, founder of Judith Jack Jewelry

That's what one of our vendors, who we used as a credit reference, said to another vendor, who was considering extending us credit.

In the early years of my retail business, I naively believed that as I had a seasonal business, suppliers wouldn't expect me to pay any outstanding balances after a season ended until the following season began.

One winter day, a vendor, with whom we had a special relationship, called to say how disappointed and furious they were that we had not paid off our balance.

I realized, from that moment on, the importance of letting my vendors know 4 things if we were behind on a payment:

1. Our current situation

2. Our regrets for falling behind

3. Our clear intention to pay off the balance

4. A payment schedule we can confidently adhere to

I discovered how appreciative vendors were when I proactively gave them a plan to pay them back, as opposed to hiding and avoiding them.

The mantra - They should hear from you before you hear from them.

"We want to hear bad news immediately, but we procrastinate in sharing it with others."

I believe these principles apply to any debt where you have fallen behind.

We've all seen friendships lost and families in drama with relatives that don't talk to one another — liens placed on assets and businesses. Government institutions place hefty fines and interest payments on companies that can't financially recover, and their credit score tanks.

Up to a point, people and institutions will work with you if you keep them in the loop and share a realistic payment plan that you can live up to. Don't make a bad situation worse.

There was one point in our business, during a difficult season, when we owed ten vendors approximately $1,000 each. We called each one and offered to make three monthly payments of $333. Only one out of the ten said we needed to pay them sooner, so we did. The other nine agreed, and we never lost a single relationship.

As Jim Collins writes in his bestseller business book *Built to Last*, "Face the danger."

It will make you stronger and show your character.

THE POWER OF PARAPHRASING

The great Peter Drucker, management consultant, educator, and author, said that 60% of all management problems result from poor communication. When employees and managers fail to understand each other, everything suffers - sales, service, safety, productivity, and morale.

It's critical to understand that communication is a two-way street. If the information is passed down several channels, it may become the equivalent of whispering down the lane.

Communication miscues happen in companies every day. No one is lazy - everyone is well-intentioned and tries their best. When we communicate a message and don't have the luxury of seeing with our own eyes that the right information is implemented in a timely fashion, it's primarily because of a flawed communications process.

The Power of Paraphrasing

In 1969, I worked on a project for The Product Company of America. They introduced me to the power of paraphrasing. On my first day, I was trained in the art of paraphrasing. During the next four months, we *never* had a poor communication exchange. Impossible, you say? Here's why it happened.

If you want almost zero communication errors in your business, try this simple and effective process I was taught:

1. Tell - Pass along information, either verbal or written.

2. Summarize - Highlight the action or significant items.

3. Paraphrase - Have the other person respond in their own words with their understanding of what you said.

4. Repeat - Answer back with acknowledgment or correction.

It may sound silly, even demeaning, but what's more demeaning than the consequences of poor communication? It doesn't sound demeaning to airplane pilots, soldiers, and operating room staff. *IT WORKS* and doesn't need to be reserved for only life or death situations.

We operated a "buddy system" at The Product Company of America where your partner was authorized to fine you $50. We understood, if we didn't paraphrase and something was miscommunicated, then whoever was involved got a $50 fine.

Establishing a culture of effective communications cannot be under-valued. We recommend that you teach everyone in your company the art of paraphrasing and make it mandatory. It goes like this: "In other words, what you just said is that everyone in the company should repeat in their own words what they just heard."

Yup, that's what we mean. Everyone should repeat what he or she just heard to ensure clarity. Ask yourself when you give a message if the message is clear and listen to make sure that it is understood.

Test drive the 4-step approach to paraphrasing and see the impact it has in your company or your world. Got that? We are challenging you to try the 4-step communication process. Please let us know how it works for you!

BUY-IN IS A TWO-STEP PROCESS

In the late 1980's I had the opportunity to work with Doug Dohring. His entrepreneurial success story began in 1986 when he founded The Dohring Company, which became a top-100 market research firm and the largest provider of custom market research to the retail automotive industry.

In 2007, he also founded Age of Learning, Inc., and was the CEO until 2019. He now serves as Executive Chairman of Age of Learning and Chairman of the Age of Learning Foundation. He was also the founder of ABC mouse.

Doug, now retired, was a visionary and knew how to run a company better than any entrepreneur I worked with up until that time. He is also an active member of the Scientology community.

To run his companies, he employed many of the systems created by L. Ron Hubbard, the founder of Scientology. Hubbard was a controversial man of many talents, including being a screenwriter for films and surprisingly creating business systems.

Doug enthusiastically shared with me Hubbard's approach to effectively run a business. I want nothing to do with Scientology, but I always respond to an exceptional business approach.

It was impressive, and I shared it with two clients who owned an Archadeck Outdoor Living franchise in Richmond, Virginia. The owners loved it and wanted to implement it immediately. They arranged a meeting with their staff to introduce the concept.

We started the day with the Archadeck team. As soon as I mentioned that L. Ron Hubbard created the system, everyone shut down. It was a very long day. It was the only time I had ever faced a hostile audience; mouths shut and crossed arms and legs. During the lunch break, no one sat beside me.

When I asked at the end of the day how they thought we could implement it, the silence continued. The next day, I got a call from the owners who said, "The team hated it and had no confidence in me." They were sorry, but as a result, our working relationship was over.

I learned invaluable lessons from the experience.

1. I should have focused on the impact the plan had on The Dohring Company and never mentioned Scientology. Where Doug learned the system was irrelevant.
2. We did not ask for any buy-in or feedback before the meeting. The plan was a total surprise to the company. We should have explained the system and shared what we liked about it.
3. Buy-in is a two-step process. Logical and Emotional.
4. The first step is explaining why making the change is a logical conclusion that will make the company more efficient or solve a significant problem. The best way to achieve this is by including the people it will impact and being responsible for its implementation.
5. The second step is emotional - to answer the "What's in it for me?" question. Will it make my job easier; will I have more responsibility; will I receive more training? Am I being set up for failure?

Reflecting on this experience, I realized that we pushed the program on them without taking the time to get any buy-in.

People must buy in logically and understand why an initiative makes sense for the company and emotionally "what's in it for me." Had we never mentioned Scientology and taken the time to explain the "why" and ask for everyone's input, the program's implementation could have been a game-changer.

Wisdom comes from experience and experience often comes from failures.

ARE YOU A CREATOR OR A VICTIM?

⚜

"Everything can be taken from a man but one thing: the last of the human freedom — to choose one's attitude in any given set of circumstances, to choose one's own way." - Viktor Frankl

A creator takes control of their life by their attitude, positivity, and their actions while the victim blames others for their failures and unhappiness. It's all a matter of choice.

A Creator:

- See themselves as powerful
- Focuses on possibilities.
- Questions their beliefs.
- Focuses on what they want.
- Creates from passion.
- Sees multiple options.
- Are comfortable with the unknown.
- Sees others as equals and allies.

A Victim:

- Sees themselves as powerless.
- Focuses on scarcity.
- Defends their beliefs.
- Focuses on what they don't want.
- Does what others expect of them.
- Does not see choices.
- Limits themselves to what they know.
- See themselves as less than others.

The choice is always ours to make—one choice at a time.

SAY YES TO SAYING NO

"The difference between successful people and really successful people is that really successful people say no to almost everything." - Warren Buffett

Entrepreneurs see opportunities everywhere and are constantly approached by others with business ideas.

In my world of coaching entrepreneurs, helping them decide what to say yes to and what to run from comes with the territory.

As I write this:

- One of my clients will complete an acquisition on Friday.
- One is developing additional software for the market his company serves and is creating an innovation division.
- Two are in the early stages of buying businesses.
- One is in the early stages of starting a new business with a partner.
- One is developing several products that can revolutionize an industry.

And at seventy-five, I started a new business last year with Moe and our partner Bob Hernandez.

Most are built to flip within five years, and a few are built to last.

Last week, I sent the above Warren Buffet quote to a client who has a tough time saying no. On our next call, he said he visited his father-in-law, an extremely wise, wealthy, and successful man, and asked him how he decides what opportunities to invest in and what to reject since it was not uncommon for him to be approached with business ideas several times a month.

He shared the baseline criteria that have helped him make wise choices on when to say no.

"If it is out of my core business,

If it is not within my long term "Wish Business Portfolio" for passive income,

If it has the potential to go bankrupt,

If it's far away geographically, like China,

If it's out of my area of expertise (Operations, Sales or Marketing),

If it does not appeal to me intellectually or emotionally,

I say No."

After some soul searching, my client came up with his list, which he shared.

"Nothing over $1M,

Only where I can have enough control and decision power,

Only when it's in my Zone of Expertise and know-how.

Those are the first filters; then,

I will screen the business partners for their core values and then decide,

Do I have the time?

Does it meet my personal or business purpose?

And is there a clear exit strategy?"

After he shared this with me, he said, "Now it seems very difficult to say yes!"

"Sometimes I say yes when I oughta no." - Delbert McClinton

AN UNINTENDED CONSEQUENCE
OF COVID

R ecently one of my clients shared their concern and frustration that four of their team members will be leaving them shortly. After our conversation, I called back and said that this was probably another unintended consequence of the pandemic.

Sure enough, yesterday morning, I read this article in Mike Allen's excellent daily column in Axios:

"1 in 4 workers (26%) plan to look for a job at a different company once the pandemic has subsided, according to Prudential's Pulse of the American Worker Survey, conducted by Morning Consult in March," Kim Hart writes. Furthermore,

- That number is even higher (34%) for millennials, the largest generation in the workforce today.
- Of those planning to leave their current job, 80% are concerned about career growth, and nearly 75% say the pandemic made them rethink their skills.
- High-performing workers no longer feel geographically tied to local employers in a remote world.

Prudential Vice-Chair, Rob Falzon said business leaders "need to get back to looking more intently at our talent and ensuring we are giving them opportunities even in a remote environment, or we're going to lose them."

- Most workers say they want to work, at least, part of the time remotely after offices reopen, multiple surveys suggest.
- Nearly half of remote workers told Prudential they'd be nervous about job security if they stayed remote while colleagues returned."

In a follow-up call with my client yesterday morning, we decided that the CEO should have one-on-one meetings with everyone in the company and ask:

- What are their current and future goals?
- How can we support you in achieving them?
- What do you like best and least about working for the company?
- Where can we improve?
- What do you recommend we do to make this the best company to work for?

I look forward to the results and the many other things this CEO will learn. Please note these questions are focused on the ideas, opinions, and goals of the team members, I encourage every company leader to ask the same or similar questions at least once a year.

RETAIL STORE FRONTS AND ONLINE SALES

"The Big Bad Wolf is Amazon now" - Barbara Kahn, Professor of Marketing, University of Pennsylvania Wharton School of Business

A mazon has surpassed Walmart as the world's largest retail seller outside of China. The shift from brick-and-mortar to online shopping has changed how people buy almost everything.

While Walmart's sales grew $24 billion in 2020, in about the same period, the total value of everything people bought on Amazon rose by nearly $200 billion.

Two of my clients, who over the last decade have built their businesses in brick-and-mortar storefronts, decided to focus future growth on selling their products online.

In one case, it became clear that the cost of operating a retail store was too much, from:

- The start-up costs
- Leasehold improvements
- Licenses
- Ongoing rent

- The cost of bringing traffic to one location
- The cost of staffing
- Utilities

And the costs go on! The company decided that growth, through additional storefronts, is a relic of the past. The business model of four other clients is e-commerce based.

We plan to start "The Coach to the Best Academy," web courses in 2022. You most likely didn't find the book you're reading in a retail bookstore, you bought it on Amazon.

Online education is exploding, and so is the competition. The same holds true for any online venture. All this being said, the cost of starting an online business is substantial and not without risk.

Not surprisingly, Walmart, Target, and Costco have all invested heavily in their online sales presence. Retail historians like Gary Hoover, the founder of Bookstop, may see it differently, but at this moment in time, I believe growth through retail storefronts may represent the past, while online businesses, both business-to-business and business-to-consumer, are the present and the foreseeable future.

SALES, TAX-FREE WEEKENDS, BLACK FRIDAY BARGAINS, AND FREE SHIPPING - NOT SO FAST!

$\approx$

I n 2018, legislation was signed into law that established an annual sales tax holiday for one weekend each year.

Massachusetts held its sales tax holiday on August 14th and 15th, 2021. They joined 17 other states that had a "sales tax-free" holiday. Most states hold their annual sales tax-exempt holiday before kids go back to school. States encourage this kind of consumer spending.

The Massachusetts sales tax is 6.25% of the sale price on products which include school-related supplies, clothing, athletic wear, and furniture.

Before that weekend, Curt Carpenter, co-founder and CEO of Lekker Home Modern Furniture and Decor, shared the phenomena regarding the traffic and sales that the sales tax-exempt weekends generated.

"We could hold a sale slashing prices by 30%, and it would not even begin to draw the kind of business the "tax-free weekend will," he said.

"The sales tax in Massachusetts is only 6.25%, a lot less than 30%."

On August 16th, 2021, the company shared the results from that weekend, and it was just as Mr. Carpenter predicted.

As a former retail business owner, the psychology of what motivates a buyer never ceases to amaze me. Black Friday sales draw thousands of customers, jamming the doors of Walmart and other Big Box stores hours before they open, often leading to customers fighting for the opportunity to buy perceived deals. December 26 has the same impact.

Amazon pressures its sellers to participate in Amazon special sales weekends by offering additional discounts with free shipping.

Customers sign up for Amazon Prime at an additional cost to enjoy the benefits of free shipping and faster delivery, even if this means that the total price of the item ends up being higher than what it was originally on sale for on Amazon.

Consider the effects of supply and demand on the market. Perhaps consider purchasing items like air conditioners in the winter, next year's Christmas gifts in January or February, and sweaters in the spring. You'll find better deals with no crowds and hysteria. Buyer Beware.

WHO'S TELLING YOUR STORY?

A client is on the verge of making a crucial financial and marketing decision.

He wants to create a brand, gain market awareness, and get in front of the people who will click on Amazon. He is not sure if this is a hole he absolutely must fill. He asks:

"Is this a vital position? Can I outsource it? Can my operations person continue to take on marketing as well?"

To help him answer these questions, I asked a marketing maven at another client's company to share her wisdom.

Here are some of the excerpts from the call that every CEO can learn from:

Marketing Maven: "I think marketing is the lynchpin to any company. I believe that you can have great products. You can have a great business model and can have fantastic investors. But, if you don't have someone who can tell your story and do it well, it's hard to compete. Without this, it's hard to get brand awareness ensuring your existence in the market for a long time."

CEO: "We've just been so accustomed to doing business on Amazon and we like that they bring traffic for us. We launch a product, and we see traffic."

Marketing Maven: "I would consider expanding your Shopify presence once you have this person. You can harvest your traffic and do media buys and so forth."

CEO: "Frankly, I don't have the attention for that, even though I'm pretty sure I could figure it out and do it. It's the difference between me doing everything myself or with a few people and bringing in experts to guide me rather than me learning."

Marketing Maven: "A similar fork happened with my company. Before I was hired, there was one person who handled both marketing and operations. She was very talented but spread too thin. I find this is a frequent scenario. Hiring people for marketing should not be taken lightly. Many companies hire kids out of college, interns with marketing degrees, or individuals with excellent analytics skills and forget about the most crucial part of marketing—a person who can design, write, and who understands psychology. That will trump someone who understands how to use the software."

CEO: "Yeah, exactly."

Marketing Maven: "So, I found that the best balance for how people function and how we function was in-house. It would be best if you had someone making your tangible graphics, telling your story; whatever it is, you're still figuring it out. It's so much better for them to come from in-house to make it a personal experience. People can tell if they're buying from you or buying from someone outsourced. It's better to have that storytelling brain. Don't outsource that; outsource ads."

Consumers care about the story of a business. A pretty big mistake companies make, especially when they're small, is to outsource. Focus on finding a talented person at writing and design who is dedicated to creating and telling your story.

DITCH THE DRAMA

BY GUEST CONTRIBUTOR MAUREEN MCBRIDE

"If it's hysterical, it's historical." - Lori Gottlieb

Recently we coached a business that had a drama-prone employee on staff. Jane was bright and ambitious, with a can-do attitude and a sunny disposition; she was by all accounts a valuable team player.

However, in high-stress situations, Jane would burst into tears at a moment's notice. She framed the story of her emotional sensitivity as an unavoidable consequence of her childhood trauma.

Her father had abandoned her, her mother, and her sister both emotionally and financially for "the other woman." In search of a father figure, the young woman became fixated on her boss as the substitute person for that role in her life and asked him to mentor her. He agreed and was wise enough to maintain a healthy professional distance as he offered her guidance in her career."

Eventually, her boss married, and his new wife engaged with him in running their business, unwittingly triggering Jane's unresolved issues.

The story played out in Jane's mind; once again, "daddy" was choosing "the other woman." The boss's new wife threatened her idea of affection and position in her substitute father's life; it was happening again! She was losing everything again!

Eventually, after months of exhausting daily dramas, Jane quit without notice. She left, hurling accusations, making veiled threats, and torching bridges behind her. With her actions, she chose drama over resolution.

If we took a poll tomorrow and asked: Should a person attempt to address emotional issues at work? People would universally agree, No, absolutely not!

And yet day after day, unresolved emotional issues, large and small, interfere with performance, production, and team alignment. What is the cost of not addressing a healthy way to manage emotions in the workplace?

Before we assess the cost of not addressing our emotions, we need to distinguish between emotions and drama. We all feel emotions. They are a natural part of the human experience - the thoughts we think and the experiences we have had affect the emotions we feel. Drama, on the other hand, is an ugly sticky charade we play to avoid looking at real feelings. **Transformation occurs when we address our feelings and learn from them.**

It helps us to remember:

Feelings are not facts, and you will be playing whack-a-mole if you try to push feelings away.

There is great freedom in envisioning your feelings as cloud formations in the sky, drifting on the winds, changing shape and size as they pass through us. This can help to remind us that we are not our thoughts, and to instead observe our thoughts as they arise in our minds with a sense of curiosity. This way we can learn to not immediately react to every thought that enters our mind, but instead to challenge these thoughts and explore the feelings that result.

Our feelings will not kill us, although trying to avoid them might!

WARNING, I'M ATTRACTED
TO YOU!

Yesterday I came across a card I tucked away in a drawer. It was given to all the students at a Katherine Hendricks' Conscious Loving workshop Moe and I attended several years ago.

On one side, it reads:

WARNING
I'm attracted to you
(see reverse)

And on the other side:

Because of that, I will probably project onto you all my childhood anxieties and unresolved issues from past relationships. I want to let you know in advance that none of that stuff has anything to do with you. Please keep this card and show it to me if I try to con you into thinking something is your fault.

As I've shared on many *Food for Thought* posts, Moe and I met on Match.com, and because she was the primary caregiver for her mom at the time, she was living in Conneautville, PA, and I was living in Austin, Texas.

From the time we connected in early September, we communicated almost daily by phone or text. We met for the first time in Pittsburg, PA, on December 14, 2012, and on the morning of December 16, before I flew back to Austin. She said to me "I think we can make this work, but I have a request. We both have been married before, and I would like us to find a relationship coach to see at least once a month for a year."

I agreed, and Moe found Cary Dodson, a *Conscious Loving* coach living in Austin. In one of the early sessions, Cary put three colored cardboard cards on the carpet. In large capital letters, one card said 'VICTIM', one said 'VILLAIN', and the other said 'HERO'.

Cary asked Moe to share an incident of stress during the preceding week, and then she guided her to move from one card to the next that illustrated where she was on the drama triangle of victim, villain, or hero. As Moe told her story, I interrupted and said, 'Hey, she's making me the villain."

Cary turned to me and said, "Maybe this is not about you, Rich." "Not about me? Listen to what she's saying!" I said, raising my voice. Cary said, "I am, and it may not be about you." It took me about a week to get it. Like the card says,

"I will probably project onto you all my childhood anxieties and unresolved issues from past relationships. I want to let you know in advance that none of that stuff has anything to do with you. "

At 75 years old, I realize that I'm still dealing with my childhood anxieties and unresolved relationship issues. On good days, I can laugh at them and myself. But, on bad days, I might need to give you one of these warning cards.

Make today the day you try not to project your childhood anxieties and issues onto someone you love.

LET TALENTED PEOPLE DO WHAT THEY DO BEST!

ast week, during a retreat with one of my client's leadership team, we assessed their associates' talent.

We agreed that all 25 people who work in the company were "A" players who do their job exceptionally well, are reliable, and adhere to the company values.

My question was who amongst them were future leaders. As we assessed the talent further, three company members were on everyone's list.

We did a deep dive into their skills and contributions. We realized that each has exceptional skills in certain aspects of their job and were not as strong in other aspects.

What if they focused only on where they excelled, and other colleagues took over their other responsibilities? During Phase 1 of a company's growth (1-10 people), the mantra is "Everyone does everything." By phase three (25-50 people), that mantra works against you. You need people to specialize in those critical jobs and take ownership and responsibility. It is a myth to think you can be responsible for one thing if you're doing two or more.

With 25 or more people, a company must rethink roles and responsibilities. Generic job responsibilities where one size fits all are counterproductive.

As you plan for the year, I recommend taking a hard look at your organizational chart and recreating it by assessing it from the perspective of what skills you need and who has them.

Decide the best way to utilize your talent pool and empower each team member to take ownership of what they do best.

THE POWER OF PEER PRESSURE

"The world as we have created it is a process of our thinking. It cannot be changed without changing our thinking." - Albert Einstein

The term 'peer pressure' can have negative connotations and is often associated with young people being influenced to do something that they don't want to do. But peer pressure can be a positive thing. It's human instinct that when society deems something as acceptable or unacceptable, we feel compelled to conform for fear of being disliked or rejected. This can deter us from actions and behaviors that could be unethical or immoral.

Here is an example from my days spent in the military. Everyone in basic training was drafted, volunteered, or served their active duty as a national guard member, with one exception. The one exception was the son of an army colonel starting at West Point in the fall.

We were all restricted to on-base privileges during the weekends of our first month. The company commander addressed us during roll call on Monday morning after our first weekend of on-base privileges.

He said, "I am only a Second Lieutenant, and if a Colonel calls me and asks me to give his son special privileges, I will always say yes like I did this past weekend. However, if I am asked again, no other company member will receive a pass for the rest of basic training."

It didn't take us long to find out what happened. The Colonel's son knew that he was responsible for 350 of his colleagues not getting a pass. He immediately called his dad and said, "Please don't ask the Second Lieutenant to give me any other special privileges." That's the power of peer pressure.

While working with Four Hands, I conducted a company-wide training session in our warehouse.

As I studied the company members' faces, I said, "We have people here from India, Brussels, South Africa, Mexico, El Salvador, Jamaica, England, Canada, and throughout the USA. Four Hands does not discriminate, with one exception. That exception is if someone is not pulling their weight. We don't have to fire them because *you* will not tolerate a slacker, and they leave the company." Our culture was such that everyone had pride in their work and a commitment to excellence. If anyone did not fit into this culture and failed to live up to these high standards, they left before they had to be asked to leave.

Peer pressure is powerful and has led to significant changes in our culture and behavior.

There is a powerful resistance to change. Peer pressure comes first, and then the laws. It took the 19th Amendment to the U.S. Constitution in 1920 for women to have the right to vote.

Thanks to Mothers Against Drunk Drivers (MADD), the concept of getting behind the wheel after drinking is unfathomable to most adults today. Having a designated driver is now an accepted part of socializing and has saved hundreds of thousands of lives.

For over three decades, it has been frowned upon to wear animal fur or ivory jewelry. You can no longer smoke on airplanes or in most public places. Recycling is a common practice to reduce carbon emissions, and the requirement of motorcyclists to wear helmets has saved thousands from brain damage and death. All of these lifestyle changes have been a result of societal peer pressure and a general consensus that what we were doing was just no longer acceptable.

When I originally wrote this post in 2020, the house of representatives had just voted for the decriminalization of marijuana with two-thirds of Americans supporting this decision at the time.

Almost 2,000 women were murdered by an intimate partner in the U.S in 2018, most commonly by gun violence. There are two issues here - Domestic violence and the legislation around who has the right to own a firearm.

The majority of the population wants stricter gun control, but our legislators have cowardly not addressed the terrible and shameful consequences of our gun laws. Besides peer pressure, we also need leadership and courage.

Make today the day you take a stance on something you believe in.

"Never doubt that a small group of thoughtful, committed citizens can change the world. Indeed, it is the only thing that ever has." - Margaret Mead

A WORLD OF OPPORTUNITY CHECKLIST

"The greatest opportunities are within." - Rich Russakoff

At the end of every year, I review "my opportunity checklist", which I created at least two decades ago for one of my favorite programs I created, "A World of Opportunity." It's not a list of resolutions. It's a list of aspirations for being my best self and living my most fulfilling life. As I look through the list for next year, my main priorities are to write several books and improve my strength and muscle tone.

It's a joy to share my list with you in the hopes it will stimulate you to always be your best self.

The Opportunity Checklist

1. Accept full responsibility for my life and my fate.

2. Make the most out of every hour and every day. (Recognize that they are gifts.)

3. Test and strengthen my willpower.

4. Improve my mind.

5. Volunteer for a cause.

6. Improve my health, strength, and muscle tone.

7. Take control of my destiny.

8. Travel both near and far - see new places and experience new cultures.

9. Save and invest money for the right opportunity.

10. Read the classics and ideas of brilliant thinkers.

11. Write my thoughts, ideas, and experiences.

12. Focus on the positives in my life and my world.

13. Touch someone.

14. Be forgiven.

15. Forgive.

16. Think creatively.

17. Replace a bad habit with a good one.

18. See the world's negatives as an opportunity for change (e.g., Mothers Against Drunk Drivers - M.A.D.D.).

19. Get away from my routine and seek inspiration.

20. Love and be worthy of love.

21. Learn something new.

22. Spend more time with my friends and give unconditional support.

23. Make a positive and meaningful difference in someone's life.

24. Become and remain my best self.

25. Be opportunity minded. Don't dwell on problems.

26. Be an invaluable coach to my clients.

27. Act decisively.

28. Say thank you.

The Six Principles of Opportunity

1. Open doors - One door opens other doors.

2. Preparation + Opportunity = Success.

3. Problems are the fertile soil from which opportunities emerge.

4. Opportunities are everywhere.

5. The greatest opportunities are within us.

6. Discipline is overrated, commitment is underappreciated.

ACKNOWLEDGMENTS

From the time I was able to walk, I worked in my parent's dry-cleaning business. My parents taught me a work ethic, how to take calculated risks, to treat employees, and to always give customers a great product. I learned from them how to deal with hardships and downturns with courage and resilience. They also instilled in me values that I coach to this day, and for everything, I am forever grateful.

I want to thank Moe for believing in me and encouraging me to write and share what I have learned over my 50-year career. Moe is my inspiration from the time I wake up in the morning until we fall into bed. Moe does a thousand things a week to help me. She has worked tirelessly behind the scenes in assembling a great team to bring this book to life, including Siobhan Casey and Lucy Martinez, who were invaluable in making this book happen.

There is an old saying that a consultant is someone who borrows your watch to tell you the time, and then gets to keep the watch. I've found that a great coach does not measure their success in how much money they've made, but in how many watches they have. So thank you to all the entrepreneurs that gave me so many watches.

This includes entrepreneurs like Brett Hatton, with whom I traveled all over the world, Damon Gersh, who I've coached and remained close friends with for over twenty years; and Daniel Marcos, my brother from another mother. I could name at least one hundred more who have made my life meaningful, including Eder Aguirre, Lynn Ansett, Briana Arenas, Bill Barker, Ty Bennett, John Bly, Joe

Bourdow, Matt Briggs, Chris Canada, Ruben Cantu, Jennifer Carey, Curt and Natalie Carpenter, Alvaro Chacon, Nathan Chapman, Lou Chaump, Marie Clark-Bob, Randy Cohen, Maria Contreras, Odette D'Aniello, Kevin Donnelly, Nicole Donnelly, Kathy Doyle, Haley Downing, Kat Edmonson, Marc Erhardt, Louise Evans, Ian Farr, Michael Ferranti, Benjamin Finkel, James Fitzgerald, Javon Frazier, Rob Friedman, David Galbensky, Steve Gerhartz, Arnie Girnun, Jonathan Goldhill, Juan Gonzalez, Libby Harvey-Fitzgerald, Eric Hirani, Bob Hernandez, Cynthia Herman, Gary Hoover, Thomas Ip, Margie Johnson, Randy Jones, Brett Kaplowitz, Steven Kapor, Matt Kaseeska, Kevin Kelly, Stephanie Konkel, Matt Kuttler, Mitesh Lakhani, Connie Land, Casey LaRose, Peter and Susan Laughter, Taylor Leon, Sheila Mahoney, Diane Margulies, Carlos Marin, Lucy Martinez, Andres Masis, Sharon and Bob McDonald, Ben Mendoza, Jay Menna, John Mousheghian, Meike Mueller, Michael Murphy, George Nadaff, Naru Narayanan, Hayden Nasir, Reyna Nebeker, Randy Nelson, Neille Olsen, Hazel Ortega, Gian Marco Palazio, Tom Patania, Olga Pechnenko, Polly Pickering, Ricardo Prieto Mejia, Ananth Raman, Beatriz Ramirez, John Ratliff, Martin Redigan, Richard Rossi, Harvey Sackett, Martin Sanders, Kendra Scott, Christine Sintermann, Jeff Stegman, Todd Stegman, Tony Strobl, Elizabeth Tan, Mauricio Ventura, Lisa Vitale, Benedetta Viti, Jigme Wangchuk, Rachel Weisberg, Kelly Winkler, Jennifer Wynh, Matt Zemon, and Paige Zinn.

I'd also like to thank Jim Woods of INC Magazines coaching division, who believed in me and opened countless doors, as well as introducing me to The Entrepreneurial Organization.

Thank you to Verne Harnish who asked me to write a chapter on bank financing for his bestselling book Rockefeller Habits, and brought me back every year to speak at the Birthing of Giants.

Thank you also to Brian Brault, who gave me the opportunity to present my Taking Your Big Leap program at EMP, which I have since presented to EO chapters in Mexico, Australia, Nepal, and throughout the USA. Brian has become a spiritual soulmate.

Thank you to Gay Hendricks, whose book Taking Your Big Leap inspired me to become A Big Leap coach.

And to the Food for Thought community, who have encouraged me to keep writing about my journey and what I continue to learn from entrepreneurs every day, I've had the time of my life with you.

Finally, I dedicate this book to every entrepreneur who has fought the good fight, experienced the blood, sweat, and tears that go with the territory, and survived to make their dreams and vision become a reality. It isn't easy, it's a rollercoaster ride, but it sure is worth it.

If you'd like to book Rich to speak at your event, retreat or forum get in touch via team@coachtothebest.com or on the website www.coachtothebest.com.